Starlight

Beholding
the Christmas Miracle
All Year Long

John Shea

PUBLICATIONS

For Johnny and Ann,
Leon and Pauline,
Margie, Dan, Bill, Harry and Gorman,
life-giving spirits in the flesh,
life-giving spirits out of the flesh.

STARLIGHT
Beholding the Christmas Miracle All Year Long
by John Shea

Edited by Gregory F. Augustine Pierce
Cover design by Tom A. Wright
Text design and typesetting by Patricia A. Lynch
Cover photo used under rights granted to Seescapes Publishing

Published by ACTA Publications, 5559 W. Howard Street, Skokie, IL 60077
(800) 397-2282 www.actapublications.com.

Library of Congress Number: 20069131875
Hardcover ISBN 10: 0-87946-322-8
Hardcover ISBN 13: 978-0-87946-322-9
Paperback ISBN 10: 0-87946-313-9
Paperback ISBN 13: 978-0-87946-313-7
Printed in Canada
Year: 15 14 13 12 10 9 8 7 6
Printing: 10 9 8 7 6 5 4 3 2 1

Text printed on 100% post-consumer waste recycled paper

Contents

Seeing Haloes
(For Anne)

Even at Christmas,
when haloes
are pre-tested by focus groups
for inclusion in mass market
    campaigns,
they are hard to see.

Annie Dillard was scrutinizing
the forest floor at Pilgrim's Creek
when she looked up
and saw a tree haloed in light.

She had caught the tree at prayer,
in a moment so receptive and full
the boundaries of bark burst
and its inner fire
became available for awe.

But seeing haloes
is more than a lucky sighting.
It entails the advent skill
of sustaining attention,
the simple act,
as Dillard found out,
of looking up.

The optometrist swings
his goggle machine before our eyes.
"Read line four."
Then he flips lenses through
    the machine

until the blurred letters of line four
snap into focus.
But if we break our captivity
to the imprisoning print of line four
and look up to line one,
the letter

E

will carry us away
with its clarity
and bless the smallest of markings
with surrounding light.

That is how haloes are seen,
by looking up into largeness,
by tucking smallness
into the folds of infinity.

I do not know this
by contemplating
shimmering trees.

Rather there was woman,
amid the crowd of Christmas,
busy at Christmas table,
and I looked up
to catch a rim of radiance
etching her face,
to notice curves of light
sliding along her shape.
She out-glowed the candles.

All the noise of the room left my ears
and silence sharpened my sight.

When this happens,
and I recognize the visits,
I do not get overly excited.
I merely allow love to be renewed,
for that is the mission of haloes,
the reason they are given to us.

Nor do I try to freeze the frame.
Haloes suffer time,
even as they show us
what is beyond time.

But when haloes fade,
they do not abruptly vanish,
abandoning us
to the sorrow of lesser light.

They recede,
as Gabriel departed Mary,
leaving us pregnant.

Have a Defiant Christmas!

In those long ago days of Christmas innocence when it always snowed gently in a starry and windless night, my parents would hustle my sisters and me into the back seat of the car and we would drive slowly, snow crunching under the frozen tires, into the neighborhoods of the rich to see the "lights."

The "lights" were the decorations that people put up on the outside of their houses and on their winter lawns. Multicolored lights would be strung over an entire house, etching door frames and windows, wrapped round into wreaths and bows. In the frozen front yard there were statues as large as small children. They were usually a mix of The Night Before Christmas and the Crib—reindeer and wise men, sleighs and shepherds, elves and Mary, angels and carolers, Santa Claus and Baby Jesus. Occasionally, the stiff, on-guard soldiers from the Nutcracker Suite would make an appearance. All were lit up so that night passengers in slow-moving cars could gawk through frosted windows and say, "Look at that one!"

But it was not these elaborate scenes that first brought the truth of Christmas home to me. It was my own home, seen in a new way, that welcomed me to Christmas.

Light in the Midst of Darkness

One Christmas when we returned from our trip to see the "lights," I pushed out of the back seat, straightened up, and saw our house, as if for the first time. We lived in a two flat. My grandparents lived on the first floor and since they usually went to bed around nine (a custom I have only recently begun to envy), their flat was dark. Our flat on the second floor was also dark—except for the Christmas tree.

Christmas defies

the darkness, refusing

to allow the outer

world to dictate the

terms of existence.

The tree was strung with lights, and their soft glow could be seen through the upper window. The outer darkness was all around, yet the tree shone in the darkness. There was no razzle-dazzle, no blinking on and off, no glitz. Just a steady shining, a simple juxtaposition of light and darkness. Its beauty drew me.

I ran up the stairs. My parents had already unlocked the door and turned on the house lights. I sat in a chair and stayed with the tree. The attraction of the tree continued for a while and then began to recede. Soon the practical took over. I noticed some tinsel that needed to be smoothed and re-hung. As I tinkered with it, whatever was left of the tree's radiance dimmed. Then, abruptly, the revelation ceased. It became merely a pine tree shedding needles on the rug.

It was only when I was older that I knew in a murky mental way what my child's heart had intuited. Christmas tries to point to an inner light, a tree of lights inside the house of our being, and invites people to come close and ponder its beauty. We notice this light because it is contrasted with an outer darkness. And it defies the darkness, refusing to allow the outer world to dictate the terms of existence. In more theological language, people have an inner reality that transcends the outer world and is capable of shining forth even in the darkest of situations. "What has come into being in him was life and the life was the light of all people. The light shines in the darkness, and the darkness did not overcome it" (Jn. 1:4-5).

Of course, our awareness of this truth is fleeting. We return to ordinary consciousness. We smooth the tinsel and vacuum the needles.

Greenness in the Midst of Barrenness

The Cherokees have a short creation story that encourages the same Christmas insight. The story is called, "Why Some Trees Are Evergreen":

When the plants and the trees were first made the Great Mystery gave a gift to each species. But first he set up a contest to determine which gift would be most useful to whom.

"I want you to stay awake and keep watch over the earth for seven nights," the Great Mystery told them.

The young trees and plants were so excited to be trusted with such an important job that the first night they would have found it difficult not to stay awake. However, the second night was not so easy, and just before dawn a few fell asleep. On the third night the trees and the plants whispered among themselves in the wind trying to keep from dropping off, but it was too much work for some of them. Even more fell asleep on the fourth night.

By the time the seventh night came, the only trees and plants still awake were the cedar, the pine, the spruce, the fir, the holly and the laurel.

"What wonderful endurance you have!" exclaimed the Great Mystery. "You shall be given the gift of remaining green forever. You will be the guardians of the forest. Even in the seeming dead of winter your brother and sister creatures will find life protected in your branches."

Ever since then all the other trees and plants lose their leaves and sleep all winter, while the evergreens stay awake.

This tale does not use the symbols of light and darkness. It talks about greenness in the midst of barrenness and associates this greenness with the ability to stay awake. "Staying awake" is standard code in spiritual literature. It means remaining aware of our life giving connection to divine reality even when inner and outer forces militate against it. Just as the light in the darkness reminds us of this truth, so does the green-leafed tree in the leafless forest.

Love in the Midst of Rejection

The major Christian symbols of Christmas also use contrast to emphasize the invulnerability of our inner transcendent relationship to God. "She gave birth to her first-born son and wrapped him in swaddling clothes and laid him in a manger, because there was no room for them at the inn" (Lk. 2:7). In one densely symbolic sentence, Luke brings out the contrast of love in the midst of rejection. Jesus is wrapped in swaddling clothes, a symbol that he is a loved child. He is laid in a manger, a feeding trough, a symbol that he is meant to be food for the world. These two symbols combine to point to the reality of self-giving love, the essence of God and the identity and mission of all those connected to God.

No matter how severe the outer world is…it cannot snuff out the light, wither the greenness, or destroy the love.

Yet this love is surrounded by rejection. There is no room for him at the inn. This exclusion at his birth is a harbinger of his exclusion by the religious and political elite of his time. Jesus will not be accepted. He will meet with violent opposition and eventually be put to death. Yet, as the whole gospel testifies, this rejection will not undercut the truth of who he is. He is the beloved Son of God on a mission of communicating divine life to people. This truth is seen most clearly in the premier moment of violent rejection—his death on the cross. These future events, this "life ahead of him," are hinted at in the interconnected symbols of swaddling clothes, manger, and no room in the inn. These symbols capture the truth of a loved child who continues to extend love in a world of rejection.

A Defiant Christmas

The truth of Christmas emerges in imaginative contrasts. Perhaps the best way to view these contrasts is in terms of inner and outer realities. No matter how severe the outer world is—darkness, barrenness, rejection— it cannot snuff out the light, wither the greenness, or destroy the love. Although we do not always reflect on it, there is an edge to Christmas, an in-your-face attitude. Chesterton put it simply and well: "A religion that defies the world should have a feast that defies the weather."

If I ever return to the custom of sending Christmas cards, the cover will be a picture of a light shining in the darkness or an evergreen in the midst of a barren forest or a laughing child in a ramshackle stable. Inside, the greeting will be straightforward: "Have a defiant Christmas!"

Of course, I really do not want people to have a defiant Christmas. I want them to have a harmonious Christmas. I want the inner and outer world to be in sync. Light inside and out, greenness inside and out, love inside and out. In other words, I wish people the full peace of Christmas—good enough health, good enough finances, good enough relationships, and a good enough, stable, non-violent society and world. As the lapel button from the sixties put it, "Parousia Now!" Idealistic as it is, that's what I want.

But that is not what we always get. Christmas arrives to find our health precarious; our careers, jobs or vocations under stress; our finances dipping badly; our relationships in need of repair; our society and world slightly insane. How can we celebrate Christmas in situations like these? Isn't the only realistic response anxiety and gloom?

But when the outer world is darkness, barrenness and rejection, Christmas is a lesson in bringing forth and responding to the inner world of light, greenness and love. Since this inner world is rooted in a transcendent love, it is more powerful than all the attacks that emerge out of both our finitude and sinfulness. "I have said this that you might have peace in me. In the world you have tribulations, but cheer up, I have overcome the world" (Jn. 16:33). Christmas cheer, when it is modeled on this passage from the Gospel of John, engenders in us a gentle defiance toward the tribulations of the world. Gentle defiance is not on the standard list of Christian virtues, but it is the Christmas gift that we all need to unwrap during one December or another.

The Christmas card for a defiant Christmas has already been written. Fra Giovanni penned it in 1513:

I salute you!

There is nothing I can give you that you have not;
but there is much that, while I cannot give,
you can take.

No heaven can come to us
unless our hearts find rest in it today.
Take Heaven.

No peace lies in the future
that is not hidden in this present instant.
Take Peace,

The gloom of the world is but a shadow;
    behind it, yet within our reach,
    is joy.
Take Joy.

And so at this Christmas time, I greet you,
    with the prayer that for you,
    now and forever,
    the day breaks
    and the shadows flee away.

Preface

Starlight

A hundred years ago when I was seventeen years old, I was a counsellor at a camp in the North Woods of Wisconsin.

I was assigned to take about fifteen eleven-year-olds on an overnight. We started out in late afternoon, canoed for about four hours, and arrived at Spider Island, not named for its hospitality. We set up camp, ate, and walked around the two-block-long island. (City kids have their own way of measuring.) Then we built a campfire and I told ghost stories about spiders. It took awhile, but the campers eventually fell asleep. The storytelling counsellor soon followed.

Can darkness wake you up?

However it happened, a few kids were suddenly awake and panicking. "I can't see. I can't see." I woke up, and I couldn't see either. The fire had completely gone out, and if there was a sky with a moon and stars it could not be seen. Neither could my hand in front of my face.

Soon everybody was awake and getting scared. Darkness, real darkness, pitch blackness has a way of getting inside you and stirring up fright. I was beginning to regret those ghost-spider stories. Where were the matches? No one could see to get them. Someone suggested going down to the water. There might be more light there. The only problem was: Where was the water? I told everybody to stay where they were. For once I was obeyed. I talked about basketball, baseball, swimming; I mocked the food and the other counsellors; I tried everything to keep them talking. However, all they were good for was a sentence or two, then their minds turned back to the overwhelming fact that they were engulfed in darkness. I could hear some stifled whimpering. We were a people sitting in darkness.

Suddenly the stars came out. Winds, high in the sky, must have blown

The way to

Christmas revelation

is illumined by

starlight.

the clouds away. We could see the water, the trees, our gear, and one another. By starlight we saw what was all around us, and we calmed down. The kids laughed and talked. I let some of them go down to the water. Others went back to sleep. I went down to the canoe where I had left the flashlight. You can not trust clouds. If they'll do it once, they'll do it twice. I looked into the sky of stars and then at the water and the island. Starlight had turned a terrible darkness into a beautiful earth. Nevertheless, I took the flashlight back to the campsite.

This is a summer tale that evokes an image associated with Christmas and winter. "Light shining in the darkness" is a symbol rooted in both Christian faith and seasonal change. On the one hand, it plays upon scriptural references connected with the birth of Christ. Zechariah's song at the birth of his son John contains the prediction that light will be given to those who sit in darkness and in the shadow of death (Lk. 1:79); Simeon says that the child Jesus is a "light for the revelation of the gentiles," implying they are currently in darkness (Lk. 2:32); John stresses the tension between the light and the darkness, "The light shines in the darkness and the darkness has not overcome it" (Jn. 1:5). However, in popular imagination, the light shining in the darkness is the star that leads the Magi to the Christ child. The way to the Christmas revelation is illumined by starlight.

On the other hand, Christmas is celebrated on December 25, a day associated with the pagan feast of the winter solstice. On the darkest day of the year we celebrate the unconquerable sun, who is God's Son. There has often been competition between the birthday of the sun and the birthday of the Son:

They call (this day) "the birthday of the unconquered (sun)." But is the sun so unconquered as our Lord who underwent death and overcame it? Or they say it is "the birthday of the sun." But is our Lord not the Sun of righteousness of whom the prophet Malachi said: "For you who fear my name, the sun of righteousness shall rise, with healing in its wings."[1]

More creative Christian thinking blended together the sacredness of the season with the sacredness of the religious feast. The revelation in nature (the sun) and the revelation of history (the son) complement one another:

The people are quite right, in a way, when they call this birthday of the Lord "the new sun." …We gladly accept the name, because at the coming of the savior not only is humankind saved but the very light of the sun is renewed.[2]

Chesterton suggested that this merger of pagan and Christian concerns was perfectly natural, because a religion that defies the world gravitates to a ritual that defies the weather.[3]

Light shining in the darkness is a stimulating symbol that can be developed in different directions. It is a compact image that unfolds in the imagination of the one who welcomes it. Stories and ideas cluster around it and work together to focus consciousness in a particular way. In more imaginative language, starlight is starburst, a bright center with streaks of light spiking off in every direction. We can stand in the brilliant center and follow a streak to its furthest tip, where it meets and merges with the darkness. Then we can return to the center and follow another streak. Playing with images is not unlike throwing a battered hat to an improvisation artist and watching her create one character after another, all wearing the same tipped and twisted hat in slightly different ways.

How have people developed the Christmas image of starlight, of light shining in the darkness?

Darkness as Evil and Sin

For many people darkness connotes evil and sin. We are like the campers. We sense it as an immediate threat, and we become panicky and withdrawn. Our knee-jerk reaction is to reach for light—a match, a flashlight, a wall switch. Darkness is more than a simple state of affairs. As the Scriptures often assert, it is a power and it seems to seek power over us. Therefore, we perceive light as a counterpower, a power to resist. "The light shines in the darkness and the darkness did not overcome it" (Jn. 1:5). Shakespeare knew the legend of this power:

> Some say, that ever 'gainst that season comes
> Wherein our Savior's birth is celebrated,
> The bird of dawning singeth all night long:
> The nights are wholesome; then no planets strike,
> No fairy takes, nor witch hath power to charm;
> So hallow'd and so gracious is the time.[4]

When the image is developed in this way, what is at stake is human hope. Are the forces of evil more powerful than the forces of good? The Christmas answer is that "the bird of dawning singeth all night long."

When people buy into the power of evil, they enter into the darkness and hide from the light. Darkness is no longer just an outside force but the inner reality of violent people. The prime target of this violence becomes anyone who manifests light. How will the light of the world respond in the hour of darkness?

It was precisely from the kernel of the Kingdom-proclamation, from the message of God's love of enemies, that Jesus responded to rejection and to the alliance of his enemies against him. These did not succeed in freeing themselves from their own desires, but they did manage to draw the sinless one who offered no resistance on this level into their own dark world. He whom they wanted to get rid of entered fully into their own world, and there in the darkness, in that godless place, in the realm of hardened hearts, he obeyed, and through his obedience and his interceding love opened anew the way to the Father out of the night of impenitence.[5]

The revelation of Christ lights a way out of the darkness, the godless place, the realm of hardened hearts, and the night of impenitence. Today we may not fear the external force of evil as strongly as we fear the hardness and cruelty of our own hearts. The light shines there also, and the darkness will not overcome it.

This indomitable aspect of light is manifested when light is most threatened. When the forces of darkness come out of hiding, so does the light. The image is not "light shining at noon" but light in the darkness. This contrast can take our mind down an interesting path. Perhaps our hope does not spring from outside estimates but from an inside intuition. If there is so much outside darkness, where does the light come from? In a letter written from prison on Christmas Eve, Dietrich Bonhoeffer suggested that prisoners, people in darkness,

Today we may not fear the external force of evil as strongly as we fear the hardness and cruelty of our own hearts.

were in the best position to understand Christmas. Vaclav Havel, former president of Czechoslovakia and a political prisoner for many years, elaborates on this evocative suggestion. In an interview he was asked the question, "Do you see a grain of hope anywhere in the 1980s?" He responds not by analyzing the world but by exploring his soul:

> I should probably say first that the kind of hope I often think about (especially in situations that are particularly hopeless, such as prison) I understand above all as a state of mind, not a state of the world. Either we have hope within us or we don't; it is a dimension of the soul, and it's not essentially dependent on some particular observation of the world or estimate of the situation. Hope is not prognostication. It is an orientation of the spirit, an orientation of the heart; it transcends the world that is immediately experienced, and is anchored somewhere beyond its horizons.... I think the deepest and most important form of hope, the only one that can keep us above water and urges us to good works, and the only true source of the breathtaking dimension of the human spirit and its efforts, is something we get, as it were, from "elsewhere." ...I feel that its deepest roots are in the transcendental...though I can't, unlike Christians for instance, say anything concrete about the transcendental.[6]

Havel is correct on two counts. Hope does well up from "elsewhere" and "transcends the world that is immediately experienced," and Christians do have something concrete to say about this transcendental source. This light in the darkness emerges from the union of the divine and the human, from the interpenetration of the infinite and the finite. Christmas is the celebration of this union and, therefore, a feast of hope.

Darkness as the Far Border

Darkness can also have a neutral meaning. It is merely the far border where sight fails, the opaque fringe of consciousness. If we light a Chanukah or Christmas candle, we immediately notice one thing. The flame does not expunge the darkness. It burns in the darkness. The haloes of light carve *out of* blackness a circle of brightness. Without the contrasting darkness, we could not see. Night is an essential part of starlight. As such, it symbolizes that our seeing is also a not seeing. Divine revelation includes divine concealment. Human perception includes human blindness. Light shining in the darkness is a realistic assessment of our earthbound capacities.

God may live in unapproachable light, but the incarnate Son of God, the Word Made Flesh, and his incarnate followers struggle in starlight, the mix of light and darkness. In some unpredictable future or another dimension of existence where time and history find completion, the duality of light and darkness may give way. Our vision will be clear and, as the classic hope states it, beatific. But this is either eschaton or heaven, the end of this world or life in the next world. However, Christmas is about *now*, about the time being, as W. H. Auden said. And now, consciousness, even enlightened consciousness, is light in the darkness.

Evelyn Underhill explores our starlight condition through an alternate yet related image of light in the forest:

> If we stand in a deep forest and look up through the branches to the sunshine seen in a broken pattern between the countless leaves, it is possible to say and to feel that the foliage hides the sky. Yet perhaps the living screen lets through as much of that pure radiance as the little dwellers in the forest can bear. We, immersed in the forest, are entranced by these shining glimpses between the leaves; with their assurance of the steady presence "yonder" of an infinite light-flooded

world. Without this breaking in, this fragmentary revelation, we should have no direct apprehension of the transcendent energy and glory over-arching us, by which the forest lives. Yet a deeper insight can learn to find that sunshine, that same unearthly radiance—seen by us in these dazzling and broken yet "religious" glimpses—as the essential life of each one of those leaves. We can come to realize that all-pervading energy, poured in its abounding richness through space—penetrating all things yet steadfastly continuing in itself, in the dual character of a given Presence and self-imparting Power. And with the deepening of our contemplation, with an ever more complete and sympathetic entrance into the mysterious process, the cyclic births and deaths of the many-graded forest life, there comes to us a more profound sense of the "otherness" of those secret forces in which that life is bathed and by which it is continuously created and maintained.[7]

What is instructive about Underhill's reflection is that the essentially fragmentary revelation can bring, with deepening contemplation, greater sight. We can learn to enter into "the mysterious process…of those secret forces in which life is bathed and by which it is continuously created and maintained." Although our sight is limited, we can push back the edges of darkness and see more and more. If we are attentive, our eyes will adjust to the light that is provided. The truth is we can see what we need to see by starlight.

This is what the feast of Christmas encourages us to do. It wants us to behold ourselves, the earth, and the underlying and supportive presence of the divine until more and more of the real enters into our minds and hearts. When this happens, we often use the traditional language of miracle. Miracles are just people and events that trigger our love and so allow us to see the world properly. Where there is love, there is sight:

Father Vaillant began pacing restlessly up and down as he spoke, and the Bishop watched him. It was just this in his friend that was dear to him: "Where there is great love there are always miracles," he said at length. "One might almost say that an apparition is human vision corrected by divine love.... The miracles of the Church seem to me to rest not so much upon faces or voices or healing power coming suddenly near to us from afar off, but upon our perceptions being made finer, so that for a moment our eyes can see and our ears can hear what is there about us always."[8]

Light shining in the darkness has the progressive meaning of making "our perceptions finer" so that we can see and hear "what is about us always." Our consciousness is enlarged; shrouded areas are illumined. The miracle may occur at Christmas, but the "finer perceptions" linger all year long.

Darkness as Preparation

Mystics often employ the image of a light shining in the darkness, but they develop it in a very different way. Darkness is the positive preparation for the advent of light. Light does not push back the darkness; the darkness is the previous spiritual state that produces light. A text from the wisdom literature is often cited as carrying this esoteric insight: "When peaceful silence lay over all, and night had run half of her swift course, the all-powerful Word leapt down from his throne" (Wis. 18:14).[9] Although this text originally refers to the power of divine judgment at the time of the Exodus, mystics have seen in it the preconditions of enlightenment. When we have turned away from the noise of the senses and are as still as night, then light suddenly shines forth. A monk of the Eastern church develops this approach:

In Russia, the custom exists of fasting [on the Christmas vigil] until the first star appears. This brings to mind both the star which led the magi to Bethlehem and Christ who is the true light. May this day also be a day of fast in our souls: let us abstain from all bad or useless thoughts and speech, and await in silence and composure the savior who is coming to us. Darkness falls. Soon the first star will rise and mark the start of a new day and of the great feast of Christmas. With the rising of this star, may the light of our Lord rise for us so that, in the words of the apostle Peter, "Ye do well that ye take heed, as unto a light that shineth in a dark place, until the day dawn, and the day star arise in your hearts."[10]

Night is about disengaging from distractions, about fasting in mind and heart, so that when the light appears we will see it.

Once this meaning is formulated—darkness as the emptying of the soul that is the precondition to receiving the birth of Christ—it is used to interpret the spiritual situation of the shepherds. They are "keeping watch by night over their flocks." In other words, they are awake and vigilant. Night is a time of attentiveness and singlemindedness. As they wait in darkness as watchmen who wait for the light, an angel of the Lord may appear with good news and the glory of Lord may shine round about them. If this happens, we will understand the mystical import of one of the most famous Christmas carols:

Silent night, holy night,
All is calm, all is bright,
Round yon Virgin, Mother and Child,
Holy infant so tender and mild,
Sleep in heavenly peace,
Sleep in heavenly peace.

The silent, holy and calm night becomes bright, and with the brightness comes the revelatory symbols of virgin-mother and child and the assurance of heavenly peace.

In this understanding of "light shining in the darkness," darkness is a self-imposed strategy. We deliberately starve our senses, our contact with the outside world, so that the inner world can emerge without competition. This is what Lame Deer, a Sioux medicine man, contended: "What you see with your eyes shut is what counts."[11] There is a "third eye" or "inner eye," a spiritual way of seeing. The time-honored mystical way of opening this eye is to close the physical eyes. Angelus Silesius, the mystical poet, wrote that at the birth of Christ, "night brought forth the day." In another short poem, he sums up this mystical approach to darkness:

> Note, in the silent night, God as a man is born
> To compensate thereby for what Adam had done.
> If your soul be still as night to the created,
> God becomes man in you, retrieves what's violated.[12]

Previews

These starlight themes—a transcendent presence that provokes us into hope, our always-limited but ever-refining consciousness, and the cultivation of spiritual sight—occur again and again in the following chapters. The chapters are not neatly divided units, nor is there a single sustained argument that proceeds from chapter to chapter. They are freewheeling explorations of the spiritual life through the images, stories and ideas associated with Christmas. This loose method seems appropriate both to the actual rhythms of the spiritual life and the uncontrollable flow of Christmas.

The spirit of

Christmas does not

submit to control.

It is a sled

gathering speed

down a steep hill.

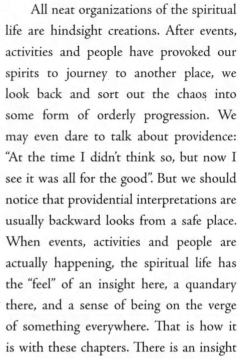

All neat organizations of the spiritual life are hindsight creations. After events, activities and people have provoked our spirits to journey to another place, we look back and sort out the chaos into some form of orderly progression. We may even dare to talk about providence: "At the time I didn't think so, but now I see it was all for the good". But we should notice that providential interpretations are usually backward looks from a safe place. When events, activities and people are actually happening, the spiritual life has the "feel" of an insight here, a quandary there, and a sense of being on the verge of something everywhere. That is how it is with these chapters. There is an insight here, a quandary there, and a "Don't you think there is something to this" question everywhere. The reflections are not a coordinated picture of the spiritual life; they are splashes of paint on a canvas. They are at that stage before the mind imposes a grand, overarching scheme. Undoubtedly, this is because I have not thought them through all the way. But it is also because in the spiritual life the mind is often the last to know.

There is a similar freewheeling character to the feast of Christmas. It usually asserts itself when we attempt to organize Christmas. All of us at one time or another have tried to plot the flow of Christmas, gotten everything perfectly in place—and then come down with the flu. The message, which we never quite get, is that the spirit of Christmas does not submit to control. It is a sled gathering speed down a steep hill. Enjoy the ride, but do not oversteer it. The feast gives itself to those willing to indulge in a four-hour meal, to luxuriate into a labyrinthine story, to rummage through an attic of ideas, to turn an image like a diamond and marvel at each slant of light. Christmas is best when we relax and let it happen beyond our expectations. The reflections in these chapters try to let things happen. They bring together Bible, tradition, experience, culture, reason and imagination, but not in a systematic way. Each element makes a surprise appearance, says more than was in the script, and then wanders off stage. Undoubtedly, this is because the author's mind is, as Buddhist thought picturesquely puts it, a "drunken monkey." But it is also because Christmas is a mighty mess of Bible, tradition, experience, culture, reason and imagination, and it is more fun to contribute to the mess than to try to straighten it out.

Chapter 1, "The Soul and the Season," explores the reality of soul in terms of the double consciousness of God and the world. These are the two eyes of the soul, the right eye gazing on God and the left eye on creation. The Christmas season tries to focus these two eyes. Through images, stories, customs and ideas we gradually refine our understandings of ourselves, our world, and the divine source.

Chapter 2, "Strange Stories, Spiritual Sight, and Blurred Guides," begins with a strange Christmas story and suggests that its strangeness is the key to its power. The many strange stories that surround Christmas try to jolt us out of ordinary physical consciousness and encourage us to see from a spiritual viewpoint. They move us along an outer and inner path of spiritual realization. However, the stories need interpreters, guides who will show us the reason for the strangeness and suggest the hidden meaning of the tale. An apology is made for blurred guides.

Chapter 3, "Waking Up on Christmas Morning," begins with another strange story, a mythic tale of Adam and Eve, filled with evocative symbols and biblical associations. Adam and Eve are on a journey of awakening. We accompany them, making our own their pleasures and dissatisfactions, their searches and discoveries. Eventually, they find a child wrapped in swaddling clothes and lying in a manger. But who is really found depends on who is looking.

Chapter 4, "Giving Birth to Christ," begins with a story about the struggle of light to come into the world. The question is how we coincide with our spiritual center so that our actions, no matter how great or how small, bring love into the world. The answer is hidden in the Christmas story of Mary and Gabriel, the virgin and the angel. Their conversation is a Lamaze class for believers. It shows us how to give birth to Christ.

Chapter 5, "The Magi Ride Again," traces the Magi story throughout Christian history. The original tale is only twelve verses in the Gospel of Matthew, but Christian imagination has turned it into volumes. The Magi have become the symbolic bearers of many spiritual insights. Poets, storytellers, and spiritual writers have explored the potential in the unobtrusive comment, "They went home by another route" (Mt. 2:12). We can go home that way too, if we follow them.

Chapter 6, "The Close and Holy Darkness," deals with the shadow side of Christmas. Christmas rhetoric has said that the child is born to die, and at Christmas our eyes mist with memories of the dead. But perhaps it is not as we think it is. Perhaps what is lost in one way is present in another. Perhaps Christmas night is not an abyss of blackness but a close and holy darkness. Love may reach farther than we know.

Chapter 7, "The Man Who Was a Lamp," is a long poem about that strong Advent figure, John the Baptist. He has a reputation for being able to introduce us to Christ. He can show us the way to the cave of Christmas. He is not as adventuresome as the Magi or as dutiful as the shepherds. But the Johannine Jesus called him a "lamp shining brightly." High praise from the Light of the World.

There are many thanks to be given to many people for this book. Special thanks go to Rita Troccoli and Wayne Prist for reading these words in their jumbled state and helping me turn them right side up. Hopefully, the results are clear and substantive explorations of the spiritual life through the images, stories and ideas of Christmas. May the words prove to be starlight, light shining in the darkness.

Just in case, do not leave your flashlight in the canoe.

Chapter 1

The Soul and the Season

"I'm not going to make it. I'm not going to make it."

It was in the parking lot of the Jewel Food Store three days before Christmas. A woman was hoisting bags of groceries out of a cart and into the trunk of her car. She was muttering over and over to herself, "I'm not going to make it. I'm not going to make it."

As I passed her, I smiled and piped up, my voice as thick as a glass of spiked egg nog, "You're going to make it. You're going to make it."

I was proud of my double assurance of success countering her double prediction of defeat. It was a voice from the other side of the aisle, a secular response as sacred as the antiphons of a chapelful of monks.

Her head came out of the open trunk. She stared at me with a "What the hell do you know, fella" look and said in a voice as adamant as a stamped foot, "I'm not going to make it."

Chastened, I trudged into the store. The "Under Ten" check-out line had twenty people in it. I wondered if I was going to make it.

The "it" in question can be many things. "It" can be getting everything done, surviving the season, avoiding a breakdown, or the modest ambition of not yelling at fellow motorists, salespeople, and—most impossible of all—your own children. On a deeper but not always appreciated level, "it" can refer to "getting into" the Christmas spirit. "I'm not going to make it" means Christmas is going to happen but it is not going to happen to me. The prescribed feelings of peace, love and joy ("How dare they dictate to me that I have to be joyous?") are going to clash with my actual feelings of fragmentation, irritation and depression. My soul and the season are out of sync.

The interaction of soul and season is what this book is all about. Soul

31

The more we know

about soul and

season the greater the

possibility the two

will interact creatively

and Christ will

be born.

is one of many perspectives on the human person. Different traditions of inquiry approach the human person in different ways. Biological traditions focus on genetic conditioning; psychological traditions remind us of mental and emotional factors; sociological traditions insist on the formative power of cultural factors. Religious traditions, while denying none of the above factors, stress that the uniqueness of the person lies in the soul. Therefore, although religious feasts may delight or discipline the body, soothe or stir the mind, fire or quiet the emotions, reconcile or disrupt relationships, and stabilize or subvert the social order, they are ultimately seductions of the soul. They attempt to bring the reality of soul into consciousness, stimulate its relationship to its source, and encourage it into creative expression. Needless to say, this is an ideal script. In actuality, there are resistances in the person and distortions in the feast. But the ambition remains, and the more we know about soul and season the greater the possibility will be that the two will interact creatively and, in the metaphoric language of Christmas, Christ will be born.

The Eyes of the Soul

"Soul" is a word that reminds us we are border walkers. We live on the boundary of the physical and the spiritual. There is "something in us that points beyond physical life, however complete that physical life may be, and suggests—perhaps in most of us very faintly and occasionally, but in some

32

with a decisive authority—that somehow we are borderland creatures."[1] Another way of saying this is that the soul has two faces. One face looks to God and the other looks at the world.[2] The *Theologica Germanica*, a spiritual treatise written around 1350 by an anonymous author, opts for one face with two eyes: "Now the created soul of man has two eyes. One (the right) represents the power to peer into the eternal. The other (the left) gazes into time and the created world."[3] In this image, the spiritual life is learning to see with both eyes of the soul.

The usual analysis is that the right eye, the eye that peers into the eternal, is the weakest and most unfocused. Despite many warnings, it continues to fantasize God as one object among many. This confusion blocks the soul from communion with the true transcendent. This is the point of a classic teaching from the *Upanishads*:

> "So tell me,'" said the father, "have you ever asked for that knowledge whereby you can hear what cannot be heard, see what cannot be seen, and know what cannot be known?"
>
> "Please sir, instruct me."
>
> "So be it, my son. Put this salt in the water and come back tomorrow."
>
> Svetaketu did so and returned the next morning. His father said, "Please return to me the salt you placed in the water yesterday."
>
> Svetaketu looked but could not find it: "But sir, all the salt has dissolved."
>
> "How does the water at the top taste?"
>
> "Like salt."
>
> "And at the middle?"
>
> 'Like salt."
>
> "And at the bottom?"
>
> "Like salt."

"My son, the salt remains in the water even though you do not see it; and though you do not see that Pure Being he is fully present in you and everywhere else. That one alone is the essence of all, the soul of the world, the eternal truth, the Supreme Self; and, O Svetaketu, you are That! You are That!"[4]

Once we begin to notice the world of spirit and to know that we have a partial home there, more complex instructions are given. How are we to relate to Spirit?

The Zen Master gave the woman a sieve and a cup and they went to the nearby seashore where they stood on a rock with the waves breaking round them.

"Show me how you will fill the sieve with water," he said.

The woman bent down, held the sieve in one hand, and scooped the water into it with a cup. It barely appeared at the bottom of the sieve and then was gone.

"It is just like that with spiritual practice," the Master said, "while one stands on the rock of I-ness and tries to ladle the divine realization into it. That's not the way to fill the sieve with water or the self with divine life."

He took the sieve from her hand and threw it far out into the sea, where it floated momentarily and then sank.

"Now it is full of water," he said, "and it will remain so. That's the way to fill it with water, and it's the way to do spiritual practice. It's not ladling little cupfuls of divine life into the individuality but throwing the individuality far out into the sea of divine life."[5]

With teachings like these the right eye opens and the person's relationship with the divine deepens.

A standard criticism of spirituality is that it has focused too exclusively on the right eye. In fact, some spiritual advice seems to pit the right eye and left eye against one another:

> But these two eyes, which are part of man's soul, cannot carry out their functions simultaneously. If the soul is looking into eternity through the right eye, the left eye must cease all its undertakings and act as if it were dead. If the left eye were to concentrate on things of this outer world (that is to say, be absorbed by time and created beings), it would hinder the musing of the right eye.[6]

Although closing the left eye is proposed as a temporary strategy, it has often become a permanent blindness. This has developed into the caricature of the spiritual person as "otherworldly" and the spiritual journey as the strictly inner activity of solitudinous people. A continual caution of traditional spirituality was to not let the soul get lost in the world of "created things" and lose sight of its relationship to God. But the soul can also get lost in God and lose sight of its relationship to "created things." Lost in God may have a more rapturous ring than lost in "created things," but it is still lost.

Today there is a massive attempt to redress this imbalance. The perspective of Gandhi is honored:

> I claim that human mind or human society is not divided into watertight compartments called social, political and religious. All act and react upon one another.... I do not believe that the spiritual law works on a field of its own. On the contrary, it expresses itself only through the ordinary activities of life. It thus affects the economic, the social and the political fields.[7]

People are talking about and writing spiritualities of gender, body, mind, marriage, work, the economy, politics, leisure, social action, recovery from addiction, etc. In other words, the created world is being scrutinized with the left eye of the soul.

Although what the left eye sees in any given situation depends on the situation, there are some general patterns of perception. The left eye of the soul recognizes the multiplicity and variety of the world, but it also spies an underlying unity. It celebrates diversity, but it does not get lost in it. This is one of the points of a training session between Merlin and the young Arthur. Merlin takes Arthur into the forest, turns him into a hawk (they could do that in those days), and sends him sailing into the sky. From the earth Merlin shouts to Arthur, "What do you see?"

Arthur responds, "I see rivers and trees."

"No," an irritated Merlin responds and repeats his question, "What do you see?"

"I see cattle and sheep and…"

"No," Merlin interrupts and asks a third time, "What do you see?"

"I see villages and…"

"Come down," orders Merlin. Arthur, the hawk, returns to earth and becomes Arthur, the young boy. Merlin tells him, "Some day you will know what you saw." The day Arthur knows what he saw was the day after his dream of Camelot died. He saw no boundaries. When he was in the sky and looking at the earth, everything was distinct yet also part of a unity. In the universe there may be many lines, but the lines can be viewed as either divisions or meeting places. Both divisions and meeting places are created by the mind.[8]

The flight of Arthur is available for people today without the magic of Merlin. Georgia O'Keeffe, the influential American painter, once suggested that everybody take a ride in an airplane. She thought the perspective from the airplane would change the way people see things. What is seen from airplane altitude is the connectedness of what appears from the ground level to be separated. Alfred North Whitehead used the same image in another context but for a similar purpose: "The true method of discovery is like the flight of an aeroplane. It starts from the ground of particular observation; it makes a flight in the thin air of imaginative generalization; and again lands for renewed observation rendered acute by rational generalization."[9] When the plane ride is successful, "some synoptic vision has been gained."[10] In other words, things are seen in their interconnectedness.

Fred Hoyle, the astronomer, went Arthur, O'Keeffe and Whitehead one better. In 1948 he predicted, "Once a photograph of the earth, taken from the outside, is available—once the sheer isolation of the earth becomes plain, a new idea as powerful as any in history will be let loose." We have gone up from an airplane ride to a spaceship ride. Although what is seen at each height is the same and so there is a continuity of vision, the perspective also changes and with it our consciousness of who we are on this earth. Beatrice Bruteau suggests that the picture of the earth from space generates the idea that "we human beings—better, perhaps, we living beings—constitute one family on a tiny fragile planet in limitless space."[11] These stories and ideas of "seeing from height" are exercises to train the left eye to see the unity of the diverse world.

As we play with the image of height and sight, we are gradually moving the left eye, which views creation, into line with the right eye, which views "our Father in heaven," the High God. The ultimate goal of the spiritual life is to coordinate both eyes into a single vision. This single vision, the working together of the two eyes of the soul, is often called the eye of God. The mystical injunction is to see with the eye of God. Chaim Potok tells us what we can expect:

My father, of blessed memory, once said to me, on the verse in Genesis: "And He saw all that He did and behold it was good" —

my father once said that the seeing of God is not like the seeing of man. Man sees only between the blinks of his eyes. He does not know what the world is like during the blinks. He sees the world in pieces, in fragments. But the Master of the Universe sees the world whole, unbroken. That world is good. Our seeing is broken, Asher Lev. Can we make it like the seeing of God? Is that possible?[12]

Spiritual exercises want to bring us to such wide-awake, open-eyed clarity that we will see the universe whole, see it *during* the blinks. "Is that possible?" is the question that entices all spiritual seekers.

Therefore, the spiritual life is, at root, a matter of seeing. It is not about sectioning out and cordoning off a part of life and then calling it spiritual and separating it from everything else that is called secular. The spiritual life is all of life seen from a certain perspective. It is waking, sleeping, dreaming, eating, drinking, working, loving, relaxing, recreating, walking, sitting, standing and breathing understood and engaged in from the single vision of the two eyes of the soul, the eye of God. However, certain events, people and activities illumine the eyes of the soul in a special way. These events, people and activities become the immediate concerns of the spiritual life; and most likely it is these happenings that we relate when we tell the story of our journey of enlightenment. However, it must be remembered that spirit suffuses everything; and so the spiritual life is simply life, whenever and wherever, seen from the vantage point of spirit.

Although the goal of the spiritual life can be stated simply—the realization of our union with God and creation—the journey to this goal is exceeding complex. There are breakthroughs, tests, false identifications, detours, peace, frenzy, roadblocks, breakdowns and sudden bursts of joy, fear, adventures and boredom. I was told of a religious pilgrimage where the people process toward their goal by taking one step backward for every two steps forward. This forward-backward movement is the humble, mundane way we tread the spiritual path. It is reflected in the myriad questions we mumble and puzzle along the way. Some of these questions are sincere; some are dodges; some are stalls; some are pleas for pity; some are breakthroughs to a new level. Why should I go on this journey at all? Why not eat, drink, be merry, and be done with it? Can I become aware of soul or do I have to take someone's word? I see now and then—how do I keep seeing? How do I open myself to divine influences? What are the most appropriate forms of prayer for my style of life? How should Scripture be used? What does surrender to God mean? How does the soul relate to the mind, will and body? How do I learn to live out of the soul? Christ fell three times, how come I have fallen 4,612 times? How are the right eye and the left eye coordinated? How can the spiritual life affect my work, my love life, and my leisure? How come the more I take the spiritual life seriously, the stranger I get and the more I don't fit in? Some days the question is, "Is the land flowing with milk and honey in this direction?" Other days the question is, "Were there no graves in Egypt, that you brought us out into this desert to die?"

It is often stated that these questions are not as esoteric as they once were, that there is a hunger among many people for the spiritual life.[13] At the same time it is also stated that the mainline Christian churches, the traditional home of spirituality, are ignoring the opportunity. They are preoccupied with internal organizational struggles and external social amelioration programs. No one can dispute the importance of these activities, and certainly the churches should be involved in them. But they are not substitutes for the birthright of religion:

> Because the soul is lost—or at least temporarily mislaid or bewildered—ministers have been forced, upon meeting a pastoral problem, to go upstairs to its neighbor, the next closest thing to soul: the mind. So the churches turn to academic and clinical psychology,

to psychodynamics and psychopathology and psychiatry, in attempts
to understand the mind and its working. This has led ministers to
regard troubles of the soul as mental breakdowns and cure of soul
as psychotherapy. But the realm of the mind—perception, memory,
mental disease—is a realm of its own, another flat belonging to
another owner who can tell us very little about the person whom the
minister really wants to know, the soul.[14]

The soul is the natural concern of religion, but when the soul is lost the churches go elsewhere—mimicking, often quite badly, other sectors of society.

Perhaps this critique is not fully deserved. I am sure many people in ministry would claim they have always tried to approach their educational, counselling and social programs from a spiritual perspective. They know the difference between themselves and secular educators, counsellors and social activists. They have not lost or mislaid the soul but merely focused on the much-neglected left eye of the soul. Even so, some questions about the relationship of the spiritual life to church activity cause uneasiness. Does your church teach people "higher forms" of prayer—meditation and contemplation? Does your church approach liturgy as an opportunity for spiritual communion with God, other people, and the universe, or is it primarily a gathering of people with common convictions? Is every church policy grounded in spiritual perception and logic? Does your church encourage people to view their family and work life in a spiritual perspective or are these major areas left unexamined by the left eye of the soul? These questions cause uneasiness because even if we answered "yes" to all of them it might not be clear all that this "yes" entails.

It must be remembered that these hard questions are "confrontation from friends." It is a message from people inside the Christian tradition, people who care about the churches. They want both fidelity to the past and relevance to the present. In fact, they often suppose that fidelity to the depth of the tradition, not to its surface manifestations, will automatically be relevant to the present. These people—and they come from the right, left and middle—have internalized "something" at the heart of the faith, "something" closely tied to Jesus' life and preaching. When they do not see this "something" in the contemporary church or see its importance jeopardized, they raise their voice. Today many ask this type of purifying question: Has the church lost the missionary thrust that characterized its origins? Have the social implications of the Gospel been overlooked? Does church organization reflect the Gospel vision of human relationships? Our friendly confrontation entails "something" I think is central to the faith: Do we live and act out of a spiritual center, which the biblical tradition called "heart," which the postbiblical tradition called "soul," and which contemporary theology calls the "transcendent self"?

The soul is the natural concern of religion, but when the soul is lost, the churches go elsewhere, mimicking, often quite badly, other sectors of society.

In many cases this "confrontation from friends" has come about because of "conversations with strangers." This is certainly the case with my question about the spiritual center. The strangers involved are a wide-ranging group of people who, in one way or another, have been deeply influenced by non-Christian spiritual traditions. Some of them are Christians who have "passed over" into another spiritual tradition and "passed back" into their own. Some of them are Christians who "passed over" into another spiritual tradition and stayed. Some are spiritual eclectics, appreciating the mystical element of every religion, philosophy, science and psychology. Some are doctors seeking wholistic approaches to healing. Others are explicit teachers of Buddhist and Hindu spiritualities in the context of the American culture. Still others are philosophers who are struggling to connect contemporary psychological movements with the mystical traditions of the great world religions. Dialogue with these people means confronting the spiritual head-on, not as a function of anything else but as a reality in its own right.

Lately I have been reading these "strangers." I have begun visiting bookstores that play sitar music and burn incense, and I have developed the bad and expensive habit of buying books with the word "spirit" or "spiritual" anywhere on the cover. When the fever is really on me, I buy books with the word "spirit" anywhere in the preface. I have found this reading a fascinating experience. Much of what I read was unsubstantiated in the way I like things substantiated; or so far outside my conscious experience I couldn't take it seriously; or not sufficiently resigned to the cynic's slogan, "Everywhere I go I take up too much room;" or "too soft" for the world I live in and have no intentions of leaving; or systematically designed to quench desire when I am trying to hype it and redirect it; or even more fearful of suffering than I am; or "too far out" in a direction that may be legitimate but is out of the question for someone who has developed as many bad habits as I have and who long ago decided his death chant would be "MERCY!"; or too glib about how social change takes place; or too simple for someone who begins sentences with "on the other hand...."

On the other hand, I was awed by the straightforward, unapologetic affirmation of the reality and importance of spirit; by the insights into the relationship of spirit, mind, will and body; by the overwhelming emphasis given to consciousness; by the person-centered approaches to action; by

42

the fierce metaphysical fight against ego-centricity; by the refusal to back down on the indispensability of personal meditation; by the attempt to explore freedom in terms of the inner person rather than the outer restraints; and by the recurring stress on compassion and love. In short, it did what conversations with strangers are supposed to do. It clarified and expanded my vision.

Most of all it forced me to reread my own tradition. I do not think I would have read the *Theologica Germanica* if I had not read Ram Dass, or the *Sermons of Meister Eckhart* if I had not read Stephen Levine, or de Caussade's *Abandonment to Divine Providence* if I had not read Eknath Easwaran. Most of all it has been the insightful and visionary work of Beatrice Bruteau that has helped me reappreciate certain parts of the New Testament and the doctrines of soul, incarnation and Trinity. There is no strict logical connection among these people. The perspective of one does not immediately lead to the perspective of the other. Yet it seemed that interest in and appreciation of my own tradition emerged out of contact with the spiritual concerns and insights of people who were nurtured in other spiritual traditions. David Toolan's remark may be too strong, but it certainly points in the right direction: "If you want to get to the heart of the Judeo-Christian tradition...then I argue that it may pay to be more than a little Buddhist."[15] Conversations with strangers may be the way we come to ourselves.

In particular, I reappreciated the crucial relationship between experience and consciousness. I had always thought that experience was the primary category of the Christian, Catholic faith I was nurtured in. An oversimple yet workable theory of Scripture and tradition is that Scripture is the record of the founding experience of Christianity and tradition is the story of how that founding experience fared as it moved to different places and through different times. Schillebeeckx has it right:

What was experience for others yesterday is tradition for us today, and what is experience for us today will in turn be tradition for others tomorrow. However, what was once experience can only be handed down in renewed experiences, at least as a living tradition.... This means that Christianity is not a message but an experience of faith that becomes a message, and as an explicit message it seeks to offer a new possibility of life experience to others who hear it from within their own experience of life.[16]

The writings of Scripture, liturgical forms, postscriptural dogma, theology, ethics, and spirituality—the whole plural and productive development of the Christian tradition—are founded on a primal experience of God in Jesus Christ and renewed through analogous experiences.

My conversation with strangers encouraged me to pursue this emphasis on experience in terms of the spiritual structure of consciousness. It is not enough to formally state, "At root Christian faith is experiential." Nor is it enough to proclaim the many enshrined expressions of that experience—"The Word became flesh;" "Christ is risen;" "God was in Christ reconciling the world to himself;" "Jesus is Lord;" "The Kingdom of God is at hand;" etc.—and then move on to grand theological speculation. Nor is it enough to spin out the ethical and social implications of these expressions. We must delve into the interior of these expressions and map the terrain of consciousness they reflect. Of course there are many different expressions and, therefore, there will be many different maps. But the strangers insist that the number of maps is not the problem. The problem is a failure of nerve, a failure to read the maps for what they are: ancient instructions to the secrets of the spirit.

The Lens of the Season

Spirituality may be the genuine concern of many people today. But why try to explore it through the feast of Christmas? If we want to pursue the spiritual life through the Christian tradition, why not study the great mystics—Paul, John, Dionysius, Augustine, Simeon, Eckhart, Julian of Norwich, Tauler, Catherine of Siena, John of the Cross, Teresa of Avila, etc.? Or if we wish our spirituality shaped by the originating events of Christian faith, why not the passion, death and resurrection? Scholars agree that these experience galvanized the Christian movement. Or if we want to ground our spirit formation in the life of Jesus, why not the Sermon on the Mount or the parables? But Christmas? A feast based on the prologues of only two of the four Gospels? A feast the tradition has made to carry more weight than it can bear? A feast so chameleon that it is reshaped by the customs of every culture of the world? A feast so adaptable to nonreligious instincts that it has been nicknamed "Dollarmas"? Christmas does not seem the most likely candidate for a Christian appreciation of spiritual life.

1. So, why Christmas?

Because I cannot shake it. Over the years I have had, as I think most adult Christians have, some Christmases Dickens would not dare write about. Christmas has been just one more day—and not a very good one at that, and I knew where to lay the blame. Christmas was a spiritual flop because my Advent preparation was so shoddy. There was no increase in prayer and fasting. In fact, there was less of both. However, there was an increase in everything else. During December I have usually been overworked, overworried and overserved. And I knew that as the birth of Christ drew near I would not witness it. I was living the folktale of Befana:

Befana, the Housewife, scrubbing her pane,
Saw three old sages ride down the lane,
Saw three grey travellers pass her door—
Gaspar, Balthazar, Melchior.

"Where journey you, sirs?" she asked of them.
Balthazar answered, "To Bethlehem,
For we have news of a marvelous thing.
Born in a stable is Christ the King."

"Give Him my welcome!"
Then Gaspar smiled,
"Come with us, mistress, to greet the Child."

"Oh, happily, happily would I fare,
Were my dusting through and I'd polished the stair."

Old Melchior leaned on his saddle horn.
"Then send but a gift to the small Newborn."

"Oh, gladly, gladly I'd send Him one,
Were the hearthstone swept and my weaving done.

As soon as ever I've baked my bread,
I'll fetch Him a pillow for His head,
And a coverlet too," Befana said.

"When the rooms are aired and the linen dry,
I'll look at the Babe."

But the Three rode by.

She worked for a day and a night and a day,
Then, gifts in her hands, took up her way.
But she never found where the Christ Child lay.

And still she wanders at Christmastide,
Houseless, whose house was all her pride.

Whose heart was tardy, whose gifts were late;
Wanders, and knocks at every gate.
Crying, "Good people, the bells begin!
Put off your toiling and let love in."[17]

I knew the lesson of Befana and vowed to "put off my toiling and let love in." But every year I hear the words of the woman in the parking lot in my own mouth, "I'm not going to make it. I'm not going to make it."

Yet, despite my checkered history with Christmas, there is always something in me that is eager. Every year, even though I suspect it will not be fulfilled, a promise stirs inside me. There is undoubtedly a theological interpretation of this heightened expectancy, but I have traced it back to my childhood. Christmas was the context of my first conscious taste of transcendence, and the memory always makes me hungry for more:

What boy pulled his stocking cap over his ears
(the unmessable crew cut beneath)
and found the pre-dawn Christmas snow
waiting for him?

The street lights were city stars

guiding the magi through the supernatural night.
The boy's holy ambition was to walk the snow
without leaving tracks,
to know everything it was
yet leave it unmarked.
He failed wonderfully
across Romaine's white lawn.
Two blocks away
the bright Gothic God
invited him into the magic darkness
where ears were bells
and nose was pine and incense
and eyes were poinsettias and golden chalices.
As was his host's custom
he surprised him,
like a gift under the tree,
and took him up past the stained-glass saints
to the vaulted, wood-carved heaven.
He told the boy he would not fall
then dropped him into Christmas.

What man now strikes the flinty past
to fire the coldness of his soul?[18]

This is not a lament for lost innocence or a futile attempt to go "home again." It is the intuition that this "Christmas space" of such abundant childhood treasures also holds adult delights. Christmas is not for children but for the ever-rejuvenating child in each of us. I cannot shake Christmas because I will not admit that growing old and growing weary are the same thing. We can grow old and not only not lose wonder but increase it.

Thomas Hardy wrote a better poem about this undying attraction of Christmas, "The Oxen":

Christmas Eve, and twelve of the clock.
"Now they are all on their knees,"
An elder said as we sat in a flock
By the embers in hearthside ease.

We pictured the meek mild creatures where
They dwelt in the strawy pen,
Nor did it occur to one of us there
To doubt they were kneeling then.

So fair a fancy few would weave
In these years! Yet, I feel,
If someone said on Christmas Eve,
"Come; see the oxen kneel,

"In the lonely barton by yonder coomb
Our childhood used to know,"
I should go with him in the gloom,
Hoping it might be so.[19]

If someone says that the child of promise has been born, we will go with them through the gloom, even though it is "a fancy few would weave in these years." We are not meant for gloom, and when there is news that the world is more, wondrously more, than our poor minds are able to hold, we cannot resist the invitation. "What do we have to lose?" our ever-hedging hearts say. But as we walk through the gloom, we know what we want to lose.

2. So, why Christmas?

Because it is a pastoral opportunity. And it is a pastoral opportunity because it is there—blatantly, blaringly, boisterously there. The way things have developed, Christmas is more than a religious feast of the Christian churches; it is a cultural event. The moment Halloween witches climb off their brooms, Santas climb into their sleighs. In early November surprised shoppers come upon Christmas decorations and cry in unison, like a chorus in a Greek tragedy, "Christmas is upon us! Christmas is upon us!" If you live in the Western world, there is no avoiding Christmas.

Among those who work in the church the unavoidable is called "pastoral opportunity." The role of the church is to facilitate the spiritual life, to show the way into the love of God, neighbor and earth that is the center of Christian faith. At Christmas time more people than usual are interested in this project—at least for a time. The regular churchgoers see it as a special time of renewal. The non-churchgoers show up and say wonderful things like, "I only come to Mass once a year, yet I can't get a seat. What is this?" People are drawn to church, a place where they think, perhaps mistakenly, oxen might kneel.

In general, I favor the generous interpretation that most people—churchgoers and non-churchgoers—go through a mild repentance at Christmastime. They try to sort out the essential from the accidental, the important from the trivial. Some people, as any priest or minister will tell you, sob terrible tears of remorse and start on a new path. Over the years I have become convinced that a good deal of this openness to change happens because they cannot get away from the season. After they have pointed out the hypocrisy of the churches, the greed of the merchants, the stupidity of the TV specials, and the general frenzy of it all, the last thing they thought would happen does. A ragtail Santa Claus with a bell and a money pail, or a lighted tree in a dirty window, or a "staticky" Christmas carol barely coming through on the car radio, or a child pushing his nose against a store window, or a crib scene outside a church partially buried in snow catches them off guard. Suddenly they find themselves swimming in resolutions. They want to "put their life back on track" or "get their values straight" or "count their blessings." The ubiquity of Christmas wears them down.

Of course, for many Christians the ubiquity of Christmas, the fact that its many expressions pervade the culture, does not enhance the feast but diminishes it. They are driven to reclaim the birth of Christ from the secularizing, commercializing culture. A Lutheran church in Nebraska has taken to celebrating Christmas on *June* 25. The pastor explained: "Nobody could hear the message in December, with the distractions of the holidays." A church in Chicago took out a newspaper ad: "Since Christ's birthday falls on the same day as X-mas this year, we'll be celebrating early. Join us at 7 p.m. Sunday, December 15." A well-known advertising campaign showed a picture of Jesus and Santa Claus. The lettering underneath read: "Whose birthday is it, anyway?"

If the angle of entry into the feast of Christmas must be phrased in this either-or way, it is Jesus' birthday. But that does not mean we banish Santa Claus. I heard of a Christmas Eve liturgy that put together faith and culture in a creative way. Perhaps a hundred children, under the age of eight, were gathered around the altar. The homilist was in the midst of them. Instead of talking, he just pointed to the back of church. The children turned around and down the aisle came Santa Claus. The normally quiet church was abnormally silent. Santa walked in front of the children and went over to the crib. He took off his hat, genuflected, said a prayer, and walked out of the church. Nothing more needed to be said about whose birthday it was.

The fact that Christmas is a cultural feast means that it is an exercise in the relationship between faith and culture. I do not think the most creative pastoral strategies involve denunciation of the culture and

51

separation of the faith. Moving the birth of Christ out of the holidays is a return to sectarianism. I have my own small story about how this endeavor might fare.

I was researching this book during a hot spell in July. From my days of reading Christmas stories to little people I dimly remembered a passage from Dr. Seuss's *How the Grinch Stole Christmas*. The library at the University of St. Mary of the Lake is extensive in the Fathers of the Church, excellent in medieval theology, but woefully lacking in contemporary nursery rhymes.

So I hied myself to the local public library and found the passage:

> *The Grinch hated Christmas! The whole Christmas season!*
> *Now, please don't ask the reason. No one quite knows the reason.*
> *It could be his head wasn't screwed on just right.*
> *It could be, perhaps, that his shoes were too tight.*
> *But I think that the most likely reason of all*
> *May have been that his heart was two sizes too small.*

This is the truly biblical insight I was looking for. But the story is not in the find, but in the finding.

I arrived at the library, found the card catalogue number, and began the hunt. I came up empty. So I went to the desk and asked the librarian for help. I have logged more library hours than most, so I was a little diffident as I pointed to the call number on the piece of paper.

"I can't find it."

"Oh, this is in our children's section. Is this a Christmas book?"

"Yes."

"It's up the stairs and to the right. It will be on a special shelf in the back. A little early for Christmas, isn't it?"

The stacks in the children section have two shelves and are only three feet high. I am six feet, three inches high. The special Christmas shelf was the *bottom* shelf. As I was crawling around, a boy of about five, barely taller than the stacks, said, "What are you doing in here, Mister?"

"I'm looking for a book."

"What book?"

"*How the Grinch Stole Christmas.*"

"It's not Christmas time."

"I know that," I said. Then I added defensively, "I'm writing a book."

I have reflected on why I told this small inquisitor I was writing a book. Was I trying to impress him? Was I justifying being on his turf? Was I trying to reassure him that I was not breaking some eternal law that Christmas stuff can only be read at Christmas time? Did I really want to say, "Look here, kid. What do I look like, a space cadet? I know it's July."

He came back with the insistence of a biblical prophet. "It's not Christmas time."

To me, the kid is right. Christmas is not a moveable feast. It belongs in December—a hodgepodge of faith, tradition and culture. It is true that there have grown up around the simple birth of Jesus Christ the extravagancies of the feast of Christmas. Most certainly, the center of the celebration of Christmas is the faith appropriation of the birth of Jesus through Word and Sacrament. But clustered around the center is a sleighful of traditions, the cultural heritage of Christmas. We do not have to see these traditions as rivals and eliminate them until only the simple birth of Jesus Christ remains. They can be viewed as refractions of the

Christmas is not a moveable feast. It belongs in December, a hodgepodge of faith, tradition, and culture.

Light at the Center. Some of them need to be modified and reminded of their place. Others need to be enhanced. But most should be treated generously as attempts to extend the Spirit of Christmas.

The purpose of the customs, colors and legends of Christmas is to make available its essential Spirit. A Christmas Spirit that walks around naked will never be noticed. It needs a sprig of holly for allure. In the search for Spirit there may be a time to squint expectantly into the invisible air, but Christmas is not that time. Christmas is a time to plunge into the visible pudding.[20] The many mini-traditions of Christmas are at the service of its magnanimous and unbounded Spirit.

The Christmas tree is an example. On the top of most trees there is an angel or a star. The tree itself is strung with lights and ornaments. Perhaps many of the ornaments are heirlooms, handed down from generation to generation, or handmade pieces bearing the personal care of the maker. Underneath the tree might be a village or brightly wrapped gifts or the crib. If we behold the tree in its entirety, we see that it is connecting the angel and star with the village, gifts and crib. In other words, through the tree heaven and earth are united. In the middle of the night while Santa Claus, God's shill, is struggling down the chimney, the Son of God is climbing down this brightly lit tree and entering into the village of the human race. He is God's gift to us. This powerful mythological message, which many think is the essence of Christmas faith, most likely will be preached in the pulpits. But it will also be symbolized in any home with a Christmas tree.

In many ways the Christmas tree is a response to Advent longing. In the liturgies of Advent we sum up our hope in a powerful antiphon. The first half prays: *"Rorate, coeli, desuper, et nubes pluant Justum"* ("Drop down, you heavens, from above and let the skies pour down the Just One"). The second half responds: *"Aperiatur terra et germinet Salvatorem"* ("Let the earth open up and bud forth a Savior"). We pray for the rain of the skies and the soil of the earth to combine to bring forth a Savior. We hope there will be union between heaven and earth. When we see the angel, the tree and the village, we know our hope is not in vain.

Gift-giving is another example of a custom that reflects the Light at the center. It is also the custom that many people think reflects the winter darkness. There is a delightful vignette about a major department store that specializes in outrageous and superexpensive gifts. One year it was "his and her" camels. Another year the brainstorm was gold, frankincense and myrrh. The Wise Men would have been pleased. However, there was a problem. No one at the store was sure what myrrh was or how to get it. So they called a Scripture scholar at the local seminary. He told them, "Myrrh is a perfume made from the gum of a tree that grows in Arabia. It was used in many ways, most notably in the process of embalming. It was a gift that probably symbolized the death of Christ and by implication the sacrificial character of all Christian living." His explanation was not featured in the advertisement, but it pointed to a truth about gift giving that Chesterton, as usual, expressed very well:

> There were three things prefigured and promised by the gifts in the cave of Bethlehem concerning the Child who received them; that He should be crowned like a King; that He should be worshipped like a God; and that He should die like a man. And these things would sound like Eastern flattery, were it not for the third.[21]

Receiving and giving gifts is not about flattery or amassing possessions, but about the sacrificial giving of life to one another.

In theological reflection groups I often suggest an exercise: "Recall a Christmas when you gave a gift and it meant something special for you to give it, and recall a Christmas you received a gift and it meant something special for you to receive it." The wording may be clumsy, but the experiences that it evokes are sharp and memorable. There have been stories about jelly glasses, cognac, foot-baths, music boxes, rings, shawls, paintings, dollhouses, etc. Every section of the department store has been represented. Although the gifts were all different, the reason they were memorable and special was the same. The gifts were symbolic of a relationship where knowing and being known, loving and being loved was going on. Is this so far from the spiritual center of Christmas when it is expressed, as "God so loved the world that he gave his only Son?" T.S. Eliot once called the incarnation a "gift half-understood." Perhaps all our gifts, given and received, are only half understood because the feelings they carry are too deep for the shallow mind to comprehend.

Trees and presents—would it be the birth of Christ without them? Of course it would, but it would not be as wonderful a party as it is with them. There is a story of a family who decided to decommercialize their Christmas by eliminating gifts. They had a meal and sat and enjoyed one another's company. It was, as one member put it, "pleasant." But another and obviously overeducated member of the family called it an "existential abyss." I know what to do with an "existential abyss": Fill it with brightly wrapped gifts, even if all the boxes contain black socks.

If Christmas is about incarnation, it is about the permeation of matter by spirit. That means that *all* matter, even, as St. Anthansius once intimated, our toes, is suffused by spirit. Therefore, eliminating trees and lights and cookies and gifts and elves and Santas and feasts may just be suggesting that there is something created that is not holy and cannot reflect the Light of the World: "As long as I am in the world, I am the light of the world." Banning the cultural expressions of Christmas may be inadvertently banning the revelation. We cannot blame Santa Claus for not being Christ, but we can make sure he stops by the crib to say a prayer.

3. So, why Christmas?

Because it is a feast of imagination and reason, and both are needed in the development of the spiritual life. Imagination is the natural voice of spiritual experience. In spiritual experiences there is an intuitive perception of the whole, a vibration of our whole being to reality. We have touched upon, just for a moment, essential mystery, mystery that remains mysterious even after knowing it. Images are perfectly suited to expressing this type of encounter. One of Chesterton's early poems, entitled "Xmas Day," suggests this dynamic of revelation and concealment:

> Good News: But if you ask me what it is, I know not;
> It is a track of feet in the snow,
> It is a lantern showing a path;
> It is a door set open.[22]

About Christmas we know more than we can say. The intuition of good news exceeds our ability to spell out what it is. But when we do speak, we reach for images, not to explain but to express how it feels to know "something" the essence of which will always be more than we can know. Although the lower can acknowledge the higher, it cannot comprehend it. Conceptual ignorance about the meaning of Christmas is an authentic response to the mystery of Christmas.

Images do more than reveal and conceal simultaneously. They express and communicate a felt sense of what was experienced. Images do not communicate by naming things but by evoking in the listener or reader the realities they express.[23] This means that the listener or reader has to have an answering imagination. The original image came from spiritual experience and hopes to evoke spiritual experience. But it can do this only if it finds a sympathetic soul, someone on the same wave length. This "receiving someone" may be ready because of religious formation, personal conflict, cultural conditioning, or a host of other influences. But inherited images sleep until an answering imagination awakens them.

Images work in flashes. We see for a moment, then go blind. All image-induced experience is transitory, beginning and ending and leaving us to deal with the aftermath. Spiritual experience is no exception; indeed, it is probably the premier example. The Christmas symbol of spiritual experience is the angel. In the stories angels arrive unexpectedly and depart suddenly, leaving people to scramble about with their new insights and commissions. Joseph is bundling up his family and is on the run; Mary is heading with haste through the hills to Elizabeth; shepherds are on the move to find a child. That is how it is with spiritual experience and the images that express and evoke them. They come and go, and we can decide either to forget them ("That was no angel, it was something I ate") or puzzle them ("What did he mean by 'reign over the house of David?'").

When we puzzle the images, the work of reason takes over. What happened in a moment and is expressed in an image we try to prolong for more leisurely consideration and develop into a complex of ideas. The excitement of experience is "recollected in tranquility." This is a process of trying to turn the transitory into something more permanent. We try to shape an experience into a structure of consciousness.[24] Clear and convincing ideas are one of the ways we hold consciousness open. This open consciousness becomes a stable way we perceive the world. It also becomes a regular channel through which we come into contact with reality. This is the work of theology, a reflection on images that express and evoke spiritual experience for the purpose of structuring consciousness in such a way that people can enter into the world of spirit on a regular basis. If spiritual experience is a door that suddenly opens, theology is a doorstop that keeps it open.

There are many different ways of moving back and forth between experience, image, idea and consciousness. A procedure that seems helpful in exploring the spirituality of Christmas is to begin with images and follow their allusions and suggestions. This way resonates with the infancy narratives of Matthew and Luke. Every phrase of these stories either evokes memories of the past or foreshadows events of the future. The birth narratives of Jesus Christ allude to Adam and Eve, Abraham and Sarah, Joseph, Moses, Esther, Samson, Hannah, Isaiah, Jeremiah, David, and Solomon—to name a few. Sometimes subtly, sometimes blatantly, the stories reprise the history that constitutes what Zechariah and Mary suggest is "the memory of divine mercy" (Lk. 1:55, 73–74). It is as if every past birth yearned for and prepared for this birth. The patient genealogy of Matthew ("Abraham was the father of Isaac, Isaac the father of Jacob....") comes to fulfillment in the birth of Mary's son. Therefore, it is possible to illumine the birth of Jesus by remembering the birth of Isaac or by recalling a story about David whose son Jesus is. The infancy narratives are dense with provocative images. Every word is a wink of the eye suggesting more. The natural flow is to let one thing lead to another.

The birth narratives also hint at the future. The child escapes Herod—but only for the present. Another Herod will be concerned about him and secure his bound and blindfolded presence; but he will be as disappointed as the first Herod, who never found him. The poor, whom Mary sings about in the Magnificat, Jesus will seat at ritual banquet. The Baptist, who leaps for joy in the womb of Elizabeth, will later shout for justice and point out the one he knew before he was born. The Wise Men from the East, who honor his birth, foreshadow the Gentile converts who will honor his death and resurrection. Joseph, the just man, reflects all Jews whose righteousness is greater than the scribes and pharisees. The angels sing, "Glory to God and peace to those on whom his favor rest." This will be the theme of the man Jesus—the living relationship between divine glory and human salvation. The stories of the birth of Jesus contain the seeds of his

The logic of Christmas is a matter of taking the suggestion, trailing the tease, completely unwrapping the gift whose ribbon is already partially untied.

full-blown life. The natural flow is to let one thing lead to another.

This is the logic of Christmas. It is not a restrictive logic, calling certain images and ideas out of bounds: "I'm sorry that doesn't follow." Anything follows. It is not a matter of unfolding first principles into conclusions. It is a matter of taking the suggestion, trailing the tease, completely unwrapping the gift whose ribbon is already partially untied. Image evokes image, which flowers into thought, which in turn suggests a story that has the audacity to bring to mind another image, which connects to a lost idea—all of which gradually changes the way we look at things. Almost without our noticing it, we are seeing in a new way. And the process continues. There is no end to it. In some ways it is like free association. The theory of free association is that it is a way past the mental censor, the jailer who keeps the supposed demons of our psyches deep in the dungeon. However, this allusive style of Christmas releases angels, not devils.

This triggering process of the infancy narratives does not stop with Matthew and Luke. Interpreters have felt a marvelous freedom to run with the ideas and images of the infancy narratives, to make connections until some substantive insight into the spiritual life emerges. This is the way the Christian mystery as a whole comes into view. Although we begin with the birth of Christ, we are not mired there. There is no necessary opposition between the birth of Christ and his baptism, ministry, death or resurrection. The events of Christ's life are different entry points into the same mystery. Nicholas Lash tries to show the difference yet sameness in the feasts of Christmas and Easter:

> Both at Christmas and at Easter it is the Christian mystery in its entirety, and not some part of it, which finds focus in our celebration. We do not, at Christmas, simply celebrate the birth of Jesus, nor only, at Easter, his death and resurrection. On each occasion...it is the single mystery of God's self-gift, God's presence and promise, God's coming to us for our homecoming, that we celebrate. If at Easter the images focus on new life sprung from ground thought dead whereas at Christmas the accent is on the dawning of a light which darkness may not overcome, yet on both occasions we wonder at the vulnerability in human flesh of God's unconquerable grace.[25]

It is through the playful process of suggestion, allusion and imagination that we move from one event in the life of Christ to the Mystery that pervaded his entire life. This Mystery is also operative in us. If we find what ultimately gave birth to Christ, it will also give birth to us. Basil the Great called the birthday of Christ the birthday of all people.

For example, there is a heart-wrenching image in Luke's story of the child Jesus (Lk. 2:25–35). The old man Simeon, righteous and devout, promised by the Holy Spirit he would not die until he had seen the Christ, the hope within history for Israel, takes the child Jesus in his arms and begins his hymn with, "Lord, now you can dismiss your servant in peace." What does it take for someone to leave life in peace? Once I was at a baptism that was held in the backyard of a house with a screened-in porch. On the porch, out of the harmful sun, was the great-grandmother of the baby girl who was being baptized. She had talked the priest out of having the ceremony in that hot and inaccessible church building. Now despite sickness and pain she was there. When it came time for everyone to make the sign of the cross on the baby's forehead, the father of the child, the grandson, brought the baby onto the porch. The rest of us on the outside watched through the screen at the wrinkled fingers sketching out a cross. Then the grandmother kissed the forehead she had just marked with the sign of Christ. We all knew more than we could say, so we let Simeon say it, "Lord, now you can dismiss your servant in peace."

When aged Simeon held the newborn child whom he called "a light for the revelation of the Gentiles and the glory of thy people Israel," what did he see? What allowed him to be dismissed in peace? The answering imagination of W. H. Auden unfolds this striking image so we can better sense the hope of Simeon. This is a brief excerpt from "The Meditation of Simeon" from *For the Time Being: A Christmas Oratorio*:

> *And because of His visitation, we may no longer desire God as if He were lacking; our redemption is no longer a question of pursuit but of surrender to Him who is always and everywhere present. Therefore, at every moment we pray that, following Him, we may depart from our anxiety into His peace.*[26]

Is this what Simeon saw? Is this the inspiration of his hymn? What we suspect is missing is actually there, and when we find it we depart from our chronic anxiety into a peace given us by a larger presence. What will this "following him" entail? The Chorus has the last lines of the oratorio:

> *He is the Way.*
> *Follow Him through the Land of Unlikeness;*
> *You will see rare beasts, and have unique adventures.*

He is the Truth.
Seek Him in the Kingdom of Anxiety;
You will come to a great city
that has expected your return for years.

He is the Life.
Love Him in the World of the Flesh;
And at your marriage all its occasions shall dance for joy.[27]

Auden's imagination has answered and expanded Luke's imagery. In the process he develops and expresses ideas that will structure our consciousness and lead us into the mystery of Christmas.

Another example of the playful Christmas process of imagination and reason might begin with what many consider to be the central image of the season—the child laid in a manger. The manger is a feeding trough, and the allusion is that he will be food for the world. This suggestion plays itself out in the ministry of Jesus, in his table fellowship with outcasts, and in his final Passover meal. At that meal, which Jesus greatly desired to eat with his disciples, he identified himself with bread broken and wine poured out. To be sustenance for others, one must have to sacrifice oneself. This delivers us into a great mystery, a mystery humans often feel themselves exempted from, a mystery reflected in Galway Kinnel's poem about hunting Christmas dinner. The poem is entitled "To Christ Our Lord."

The legs of the elk punctured the snow's crust
And wolves floated lightfooted on the land
Hunting Christmas elk living and frozen:
Inside snow melted in a basin, and a woman basted
A bird spread over coals by its wings and head.

Snow had sealed the windows; candles lit
The Christmas meal. The Christmas grace chilled
The cooked bird, being long-winded and the room cold.
During the words a boy thought, is it fitting
To eat this creature killed on the wing?

He had killed it himself, climbing out
Alone on snowshoes in the Christmas dawn,
The fallen snow swirling and the snowfall gone,
Heard its throat scream as the gunshot scattered,
Watched it drop, and fished from the snow the dead.

He had not wanted to shoot. The sound
Of wings beating into the hushed air
Had stirred his love, and his fingers
Froze in his gloves, and he wondered,
Famishing, could he fire? Then he fired.

Now the grace praised his wicked act. At its end
the bird on the plate
Stared at his stricken appetite.
There had been nothing to do but surrender,
To kill and to eat; he ate as he had killed, with wonder.

At night on snowshoes on the drifting field
He wondered again, for whom had loved stirred?
The stars glittered on the snow and nothing answered.
Then the Swan spread her wings, cross of the cold north,
The pattern and mirror of the acts of earth.[28]

We may be caught up in a universal law of sacrifice. This sounds like a grim and less-than-gracious view of reality. But perhaps there is a positive side to it, perhaps in giving ourselves there is more gain than loss:

> We do believe that life itself can be sacrificed for values higher than life, but this does not mean that all sacrifice runs counter to life and achievement. There is a form of sacrifice which is a free renunciation of one's own vital abundance, a beautiful and natural overflow of one's forces. Every living being has a natural instinct of sympathy for other living beings, which increases with their proximity and similarity to himself. Thus we sacrifice ourselves for beings with whom we feel united and in solidarity, in contrast to everything "dead." This sacrificial impulse is by no means a later acquisition of life, derived from originally egoistic urges. It is an original component of life and precedes all those particular "aims" and "goals" which calculation, intelligence and reflection impose upon it later. We have the urge to sacrifice before we ever know why, for what, and for whom! Jesus' view of nature and life, which sometimes shines through his speeches and parables in fragments and hidden allusions, shows quite clearly that he understood this fact.[29]

If sacrifice is a prerational drive originally built into human nature, where does it come from? Perhaps from contact with a Reality whose essence is self-donation, from contact with a Reality who cannot but pour itself out and break itself open, from contact with a Reality who would be no place more at home than in a manger.

In one sense, our minds and imaginations have traveled a long way from the manger. In another sense, the manger was always with us, guiding our reflection. We could continue, linking images, stories and ideas until more and more insight into the world of self-giving emerges and the left eye of the soul becomes luminous. (A man once told me that when he saw his newborn daughter for the first time, he blurted out, "I could die for you." The nurse on duty said that was a little morbid. The man was embarrassed, but he felt it was the right thing to say.) This imaginative and suggestive process of Christmas can enrich the spiritual life and bring us, glimpse by glimpse, into the light that shines in the darkness: starlight.

The Premise

Recently I attended a meeting on the future of Catholic schools. The conversation circled around personnel, money, and alternate forms of passing on the faith to young people. In the middle of this heated discussion a woman spoke passionately about the spiritual hunger of adults. Her point was that if the church spoke to the spiritual needs of adults it would be creating the context for the spiritual growth of children. No one refuted what she said, but no one saluted either. I suspect the hesitancy was not over the assumption of an intimate connection between adults and children. The hesitancy was over her assumption that vast numbers of adults were spiritually hungry.

She is not alone on her soapbox. Many people share it. The current cultural situation of America is often cited as the precipitating cause of this new spiritual awareness. Some of the forces that have pushed Americans into spiritual need are the failure of technology to bring happiness along with lasers and computers, the sterility of a totally secular outlook, the attraction of person-centered Eastern spiritual practices, a new sense of kinship with the earth, economic uncertainty, the search for a transcendent grounding for the long-term and difficult commitment to social justice, increased scientific knowledge that leads into mystery rather than away from it, the generic spirituality that pervades self-help groups, especially those concerned with addictions, and in general the hardness of life and the sense that only a person with a stable center will endure and flourish. If we want to check out this assumption of spiritual hunger, some sociological studies are available and more are in the making.

This book assumes there is some validity to this cultural analysis. But all cultural analysis does is suggest that now is an appropriate time. Or, in the clever phrase of Michael Leach regarding spirituality, this is an idea whose time has come *again*. However, the arrogance of a theological interpretation of the human person is that it maintains that we are spirit-suffused whether we know it or not. If cultural forces configure in such a way that they bring this truth into the open, so much the better. More people have the opportunity to coincide with their true identity. It also means that religious traditions should make available their vast resources of spiritual perspectives and practices. This moment is not an "unprecedented opportunity for the churches." It is an unprecedented opportunity for people, and the churches may be helpful. They are the repositories of the spiritual treasures of the past. Now may be the time to bring them out and spread them on the earth to feed the hungry.

What treasures will be brought out? What has the power to evoke, explore and nurture our souls? What will guide us into a deeper identity, a sense of self in communion with God, neighbor and universe? Why not notice and reinterpret what is present before we reach for what is absent? If there is a spiritual hunger, why not feed it with what is available? Every December there rolls around, like it or not, the Christian cultural feast of Christmas. As adherents of other religious traditions will tell you, you can run but you cannot hide: it is everywhere. As even nominal Christians will tell you, there seems to be a powerful pull, an undertow that drags you into the deep waters of Christmas where worship naturally happens. Among spiritual seekers Christmas may have a mixed reputation, but it also has unlimited potential. Can a feast that strings lights over the entire world not have the power to illumine the dark spaces of our souls? As Jesus might have said, "The feast of Christmas is prepared. The invitations are out. Who are so busy they cannot come?"

Chapter 2

Strange Stories, Spiritual Sight, And Blurred Guides

In thirteenth-century Italy there was a small city nestled in the foothills of a great mountain.

It was a city of considerable beauty and the people were very proud of it. They had piazzas with wonderful fountains, restaurants with wonderful food, churches with wonderful spires, and civic buildings with wonderful sculptures.

Whenever anyone from this city traveled—to Florence or Venice or Rome—their dress would stand out, for in those days people from different places wore slightly different clothing.

People would say to them, "Strangers, where are you from?"

They would pull themselves to full stature, stand their ground, and say. "*WE? WE* are from Gubbio."

That is the way they answered—proud, defiant—and that is the way they were.

Now it came to pass that one night out of the woods on one side of Gubbio, out of the deep and dark woods of Gubbio, there came a shadow.

The shadow moved through the streets of Gubbio, going up this street and prowling down that alley. Until the shadow found someone, and then it pounced.

In the morning the people of Gubbio found a mangled, gnawed body—the bones broken, the clothing in shreds. That was all that was left. They gathered around the remains. Many could not look.

One man spoke in anger. "How could this happen in Gubbio?"

A reply was quick in coming, "It must have been a stranger, someone passing through, who did this horrible thing."

Everyone nodded their heads. That was most surely it.

Nevertheless, that night the people of Gubbio locked their doors and stayed inside. No one left their homes to walk the beautiful streets of Gubbio. No one, that is, except one woman.

In the morning they found her body—mangled, gnawed, the bones broken, the clothing in shreds. The people gathered around the remains, their anguished voices going back and forth, "How could this happen?" followed quickly by, "It must have been a stranger."

Then an old woman spoke up, "I saw it." All went silent.

"It was late last night. I could not sleep. I went to my window and pushed back the curtain. I saw in the dim light the moon provided, loping down the street, blood dripping from his mouth—a wolf. A large, lean grey wolf."

All through the day that was the talk—in the piazzas, in the fields, in the shops, in the restaurants, in the churches, in the homes. There is a wolf in Gubbio.

Two young men heard it and a plan formed.

One said, "Those who kill the wolf will make a name for themselves."

"You are right, my friend," replied the other. "And the people will be grateful.'"

"We have swords, do we not?" They smiled.

So that night they prowled the streets of Gubbio to find the wolf. But the wolf found them before they found the wolf.

In the morning their bodies were on the street—mangled, gnawed, the bones broken, the clothes in shreds.

Now the people of Gubbio were terrified.

They gathered in the piazza in the center of the city. Many were shouting, their voices climbing over one another. "How could this be?" exclaimed some; "This is what we must do..." schemed others. Finally, a man was loud enough to silence the others.

"We must bring in the soldiers," he said. "They have numbers and experience. They will be able to rid us of this wolf."

The voice of a merchant immediately countered his: "Never! If we bring in the army, everyone will know we have a wolf in Gubbio. Our prestige, our commerce, our tourism will be hurt."

Everyone recognized the wisdom of this, and they were silent.

In the silence a small girl spoke. She said that she had heard of a holy man in a neighboring city who spoke to animals. Perhaps he could come here and speak to the wolf.

The people laughed.

An old man waited for their laughter to stop, and then he said that he too had heard of a holy man who spoke to animals and he thought it would be a good idea to see what he could do. "Besides," he finished, "does anyone have a better idea?"

A delegation was quickly formed and commissioned to go to the neighboring city and find this holy man and tell him...tell him...tell him what?

"Tell him," said one person, "To tell the wolf to keep the commandments, especially the commandment that says, 'Thou shalt not kill.'"

"No," said another. "It is not enough to tell the wolf what not to do. You must appeal to the best in him. Tell him to keep the great commandments, the ones Christ taught, to love God and neighbor."

"My friends," said the butcher, "a wolf is a wolf is a wolf. There will be no change. Tell the holy man to tell the wolf to go someplace else."

71

The people applauded this suggestion and began to shout out places where the wolf might go: "Tell the wolf to go to Perugia. They deserve a wolf in Perugia. Or Spoletto. In Spoletto, they would not even know the wolf was there." There was no shortage of suggestions; most of the cities of Italy were named.

Finally, the delegation said that they must be on their way. They would tell the holy man of everyone's concerns. They left immediately, but they did not go the short way past the woods where the wolf lived. They took the long way.

When they arrived at the city of the holy man, everyone was at the noon market, milling around the piazza. They asked a man if there was a holy man in this city who had the reputation of talking to animals. The man said, matter-of-factly, that there was and that you could find him on the outskirts. He and some of his friends were fixing up an old church. The men would take them there.

So the delegation from Gubbio followed the man to the edge of the city. He pointed to a group of brown-robed men wrestling with bricks and mortar and said, "There, the one in the middle, laughing, that's him."

The delegation saw a man in a soiled brown robe. A young man, much too young to be a holy man. And worse. He was short, much too short to be a holy man.

But they had come this far.

They approached him and told him their tale of terror. They pleaded with him to come to Gubbio and tell the wolf to keep the commandments, especially the one that says, "Thou shalt not kill," and to keep Christ's great commandments of loving God and neighbor, and to go to Perugia. The delegation had settled on Perugia.

The holy man listened and told them to go home. He would see what he could do.

The delegation left immediately. But they did not take the short way, past the woods where the wolf lived. They took the long way and arrived home just as the sun was beginning to set. They locked their doors.

As the last of the sun left the sky, the holy man stood on the edge of the woods. When there was no sun at all, he entered the woods. The floor of the forest cracked and broke under his steps, and soon he found himself deep in the heart of the woods. There was no light there, and since he could not see with his eyes, he simply closed them and went forward. Finally, he stopped. He knew that if he but put out his hand, he would touch the wolf. He said, "Brother Wolf."

In the morning when the people awoke and went into the piazza, they found the holy man standing next to the fountain. They quickly gathered around him and began to shout, "Did you tell the wolf to keep God's commandments, especially the one that says, 'Thou shalt not kill?' Did you tell him to keep Christ's great commandments to love God and neighbor? And did you tell him to go to Perugia?"

The people so surrounded the holy man that no one could see him, for he was very short. So he climbed the three steps of the fountain, and with the water springing up behind him he said nothing, only smiled. Finally, the people quieted down and he spoke.

"My good people of Gubbio, the answer is very simple. You must feed your wolf."

With that he descended the fountain, the people parted, he walked through them, and he returned to his own city.

The people of Gubbio were furious. They shouted to one another, "What does he mean *our* wolf? This is not *our* wolf. We did not ask this wolf to come to Gubbio." All day long—on the streets, in the churches, in the fields, in the shops, in the restaurants, in the homes—people asked, "What does he mean, 'We must feed our wolf'?" At night they locked their doors.

That night, out of the woods, came the shadow. It prowled down this street and up that alley. It loped across a square, disappeared through an archway. Then it turned down a narrow street. Suddenly a door opened. Light streamed out from the inside. It illumined the dark street and a hand pushed a platter of food into the light. The shadow came to the offering, looked up into the light with burning eyes, and ate the food.

The next night—out of the woods came the shadow. It prowled down this street and up that alley. It loped across a square, disappeared through an archway. Then it turned down a narrow street. Suddenly a door opened. Light streamed out from the inside. It illumined the dark street and a hand pushed a platter of food into the light. The shadow came to the offering, looked up into the light with burning eyes, and ate the food.

It was not long before every man, woman and child in Gubbio had fed their wolf.

Now the people of Gubbio still traveled from city to city in Italy. Their distinctive dress still called attention to themselves, and people would ask, "Strangers, I do not know your clothes. Where are you from?"

They would reply simply, "We are from Gubbio."

The response was quick in coming and often accompanied by a sneer. "Gubbio? Gubbio? We hear you have a wolf in Gubbio."

They would smile and say, "Yes, we have a wolf in Gubbio. And we feed our wolf."

Now as for the holy man, of course, he was Francis of Assisi. And if you go to Assisi, they will tell you that the same year Francis taught the people of Gubbio how to feed their wolf he began the tradition of the Christmas crib and celebrating midnight Mass around it. It took place on the land of John of Greccio. The legend says that, although to normal eyes the manger was empty, John saw a sleeping infant. But when Francis preached on the birth of Christ, the infant opened his eyes. When Bonaventure, a follower of Francis, heard this, he said, "It was as if the child had finally been awakened after a thousand years."

Now at that first Christmas crib, they tell us, there were many people drawn by Francis's simplicity. Also, of course, there were animals. There were sheep, cows, dogs, a donkey or two, and, they tell us, at that first Christmas crib there was also a wolf.

Entertaining Strangeness

Perhaps the best title for this story might be, "How St. Francis Taught the People of Gubbio to Feed Their Wolf." I first heard it from Bob Wilhelm,[1] and since then I have told it to many groups. Naturally I have changed much of the wording and added details here and there, but the basic structure remains the same. When Bob engages people with this story, he will often begin the post-story sharing with the question, "What image sticks with you?" Bob is leery of a premature push to meaning. He wants to stay on the imaginative level as long as possible. The imagination is the ground floor, the space closest to the earth, the place where hidden depths first appear.

When I tell the story, I too call out the images. But, unrepentant intellectual that I am, I also ask for the meanings. I go from the ground to the first floor. As always, the responses are diverse. Some are indebted more to the mood and moment of the listener than to the structure of the story. Actual listeners do not always follow the twists and turns of the plot to its conclusion. They latch onto a part and develop it according to their needs or interests. These random and piecemeal responses are legitimate, but they do not take advantage of the transformative power of the story. Other responses are the result of following the full flow of the story, paying close attention to its directive energy. When these people talk, their speech is usually tentative and reaching. They are in a meditative state, and I can see that my question is more a bother than a help. Something is going on inside them that needs time to mature.

The strangeness in

story is a seed that

grows into a change

of awareness.

They are entertaining the strangeness of the story and allowing it to restructure their consciousness.

For most listeners the people of Gubbio are only too familiar. They are proud of their city to the point of being haughty. When something goes wrong, they immediately blame it on strangers. When it becomes obvious they have a wolf, their first response is to refuse to acknowledge it because it will hurt their prestige. Their strategies for the holy man continue this denial. He should preach at the wolf and send it someplace else. The wolf himself is a wonderfully vague image that can stand for any negative parts of ourselves or our society that we refuse to face. What the holy man does contrasts with their attitudes and behaviors. He calls the wolf "brother" and suggests that the townspeople feed and not fight off *their* wolf. They immediately resist the suggestion that it is *their* wolf. But at night, slowly and one by one, they befriend and feed what they fear, and they finally arrive at an identity that incorporates rather than excludes *their* wolf. They come to this new and healthier self-understanding because, despite a surface denial, they pondered the strange strategy of the holy man. The strangeness in story is a seed that grows into a change of awareness.

We call stories strange when we cannot understand the characters and plot on our terms, the terms of our present understanding of how the world works. We are tempted to ridicule and dismiss the story. We will complain that the plot is unrealistic, that the motivation of the characters is never clear, that the dialogue comes from nowhere and is fragmented, that the descriptions are either too sparse or too surrealistic, and that the ending is confusing. But if for a moment we give the benefit of the doubt to the story, its strangeness may show us some things we have been missing and a new way to handle some of our problems. Perhaps we do not have to send our wolf to Perugia?

Spiritual masters love strange stories. They use them as tools for dismantling and remantling the consciousness of their disciples. Once I was having a conversation with a fellow spiritual seeker and, I would say, a spiritual master for many people. We were talking about discipleship and following a master. Suddenly he told me a story. If memory serves, this is how it goes:

An advanced disciple came to his master at midnight. He was very distraught.

"Master, I need to talk to you immediately. I am filled with anxiety."

"Right this way," said the master. The master opened a door that led down a long corridor. It was unlit, but the master had a candle in his hand.

"You go first," said the master.

As the disciple moved down the corridor, the master blew out the light.

The master looked at me and saw I didn't get it. "Think about it," he said. Although I was tempted to dismiss it as a sadistic encounter with a misguided master, I did ponder it, and slowly a new understanding of spiritual direction began to emerge. Taking seriously the strangeness in the story forced me to think in a new way.

Many stories of Christmas have strange elements in them that are meant to be catalysts for consciousness. One type is exemplified by "How St. Francis Taught the People of Gubbio to Feed Their Wolf." The people in the story are confronted by a person or event that they cannot under-stand in their present state of consciousness. We are meant to identify with them in their quandary and struggle along with them in their efforts to "see in a new way." Another type of story does not have characters who are confused, but for the listeners the characters and plot are not easily assimilated into their worldview. Something must change in us in order for the story to be favorably received. It is often claimed that the parables of Jesus mix and match both these types of strange stories. Therefore, it should not be too surprising that the first episode in the infancy narrative of the Gospel of Matthew urges us to embrace strangeness as a fundamental way of understanding the Christian revelation.

The opening line is straightforward enough: "The story of the origin of Jesus Christ, son of David, son of Abraham." Then there follows a storyteller's delight—endless begettings with enough skullduggery in the list of begetters for many a wink and raised eyebrow. "Abraham begat Isaac, Isaac begat Jacob...David begat Solomon, Solomon begat Rehoboam...Abiud begat Eliakim, Eliakim begat Azor...." Three general groupings are mentioned—patriarchs, kings and unknowns—all leading up to Joseph and Mary. Many people in Israel's sacred history have been left out. For example, the saintly Joseph is left out and the not-so-saintly Judah is included. The Exile is included and the Exodus left out. On the whole this is not a predictable genealogy.[2]

It becomes even less predictable and more strange when we notice the women who are included. Tamar, Rahab, Ruth, and the wife of Uriah (Bathsheba) are all women who are sexually suspect. "All...had a marital history that contained elements of scandal and scorn; they were enterprising instruments, however, of God's spirit in continuing the sacred line of the Messiah."[3] The strangeness in this opening genealogy seems to be intent on undercutting any understanding of sacred history as comprised of pious do-gooders. The divine purposes are worked

78

out through all sorts of people. If we "chew" on the strangeness of this genealogy, we may not be too quick to divide the world into saints and sinners. And we may be more open to what we might otherwise rashly reject. Even the family tree of the Messiah has a few horsethieves.

All this is a lead-in to the scandalous conditions of Jesus' birth. Mary is found to be pregnant before she has lived with Joseph. Joseph, who is a just man, decides to divorce her quietly. In other words, he will put her out of his life. He is not open to the scandal, but the angel who appears to him entreats him not to fear scandal. He should take Mary into his home as his wife. What looks like scandal is really the work of the Holy Spirit. This is a truly appropriate conception story for Jesus, a man who when he grows up will scandalize everyone. His understanding of God, salvation, mission, nation and self will sound strange and disloyal to many people and be met by ripped robes and murderous plots. What is sown in scandal is harvested in scandal. This opening genealogy and conception episode tries to drive home the proper attitude toward the strange and the scandalous: do not be afraid to take it into your home.

We should take seriously this directive from the first story of the first Gospel. Entertaining strangeness may be welcoming the Holy Spirit. In the stories that surround Christmas there are many moments of strangeness. People say and do things that make us ponder the nature of God, the identity of Christ, the real reason we give gifts, the ways of love, our relationship to those we do not know, our desire for possessions, how we eat with one another, our attitude toward the dead, etc. But there is also a basic strangeness, an agenda that all genuine Christmas stories carry. Their strangeness is in the service of an overriding spiritual ambition.

From Physical to Spiritual Consciousness

The spiritual ambition of strange stories is to move the reader or listener from identification with surface, physical consciousness (which is presumed to be a true but partial viewpoint) to deeper, spiritual consciousness (which is presumed to be a fuller, more complete viewpoint). Gary Zukav has tried to rework this crucial distinction of all religious traditions in terms of five-sensory and multisensory humans:

> We are evolving from five-sensory humans into multisensory humans. Our five senses, together, form a single sensory system that is designed to perceive physical reality. The perceptions of a multisensory human extend beyond physical reality to the larger dynamical systems of which our physical reality is a part. The multisensory human is able to perceive, and to appreciate, the role that our physical reality plays in a larger picture of evolution and the dynamics by which our physical reality is created and sustained. This realm is invisible to the five-sensory human. It is in this invisible realm that the origins of our deepest values are found.[4]

Spiritual stories attempt to bring to awareness this invisible realm by *not* making complete sense in the realm of the five senses and its unvarying logic. They are strange to physical consciousness but luminous to spiritual consciousness.

Physical consciousness is a large part of what some thinkers call "consensus trance." This is the culturally conditioned awareness we call "normal," the baseline consciousness that structures our waking life. To accept this rendition of things is to adjust; to question this framework of awareness is to be "weird'" or "unreal." If you talk about spiritual consciousness for any length of time, the common response will be "now back to earth—earth to Jack, come down." That is exactly correct. The earth is the home territory of physical consciousness, which is the "obvious and acceptable" way of perceiving reality. But from the point of view of spiritual consciousness, physical consciousness wears blinders.

William Irwin Thompson has a startling image of constricted physical consciousness:

> We are like flies crawling across the ceiling of the Sistine Chapel. We cannot see what angels and gods lie underneath the threshold of our perceptions. We do not live in reality; we live in our paradigms, our habituated perceptions, our illusions we share through culture we call reality, but the true reality of our condition is invisible.[5]

Physical consciousness is not weak in what it sees. The flies do pick up something of the Sistine Chapel. It is weak in what it fails to see—the panoramic view of history and creation.

Beatrice Bruteau suggests a metaphor that distinguishes yet relates physical and spiritual consciousness. In the lyrics of a Christmas hymn to Mary, "Behold the mystical rose."[6] If you envision the petals of a rose, they are separate at the tips. But if you follow the petals downward, you will notice that they overlap and finally are united in a common center. This line of vision represents the continuum of physical (tip) consciousness and spiritual (overlapping and unity) consciousness. Tip consciousness with its emphasis on separateness is not wrong, but it is incomplete. Our problem comes when we identify with the tip. "What happens is that we have a kind of 'short circuit' in our self-consciousness. The full petal represents total consciousness, but our *reflexive* consciousness, our consciousness of being conscious—and consequently what we consider to be our 'self' —takes in only the tip and thinks that's all there is."[7] There is more to reality than the tip, and therefore it is literally short-sighted to stop at the top of the rose and not consider its overlapping development and final unity. Spiritual consciousness views the whole rose, noticing separateness, overlapping and unity. At times it is important to contrast physical and spiritual reality and the structures of awareness that attend to them. But

81

it is equally important that any differentiation of the physical and the spiritual be placed in the context of a more fundamental connectedness.

It is this "more fundamental connectedness" that the feast of Christmas celebrates. The spiritual suffuses the physical and turns it into a medium of revelation. This makes paradox the order of Christmas day and gives preachers a chance at eloquence. Very few measure up to St. John Chrysostom:

> *What shall I say! How shall I describe this Birth to you? For this wonder fills me with astonishment. The Ancient of Days has become an infant. He who sits upon the sublime and heavenly throne, now lies in a manger. And He Who cannot be touched, Who is simple, without complexity, and incorporeal, now lies subject to the hands of people…. God is now on earth and man in heaven; on every side all things commingle.*[8]

"All things commingle" is not only the rhetoric of preachers. It is a staple of Christian theological reflection on the incarnation. Dietrich Bonhoeffer welds an unbreakable connection between the spiritual and the physical:

> *In Christ we are offered the possibility of partaking in the reality of God and in the reality of the world, but not in the one without the other. The reality of God discloses itself only by setting me entirely in the reality of the world, and when I encounter the reality of the world it is always already sustained, accepted and reconciled in the reality of God. This is the inner meaning of the revelation of God in the man Jesus Christ.*[9]

The one-liner attributed to marital union can certainly be applied to the relationship between the spiritual and the physical: "What God has joined together, let no man tear apart."

The Outer and Inner Paths

Yet just how are the physical and spiritual joined together? And, more to our purposes, how does this commingling enter into human consciousness?

The feast of Christmas suggests two complementary ways. The first, and more traveled, is an outer path that begins with an intuition that something is lurking behind the physical world and can, "if the wind is right," end with a revelation of that hidden presence. This approach begins by looking out at the world and engaging in some detective work. We pick up clues in the physical world that more is present than "meets the eye." As Gandhi once said, "When I admire the wonder of a sunset or the beauty of the moon, my soul expands in worship of the creator."[10] The outer world draws us out of ourselves into an altered state of consciousness, a consciousness of the spiritual context of the physical world. What draws us out can be the vast sky or the Grand Canyon or the soft fingernails of a baby or the cathedral at Chartres or...

It has been my habit to look at my children's feet when they are sleeping. This has helped me to cultivate an awareness of their uniqueness, their God-givenness, and to disarm myself of the posture of defensiveness and combativeness that I have created in myself. There are three different sets of feet, each perfect, each expressive of the lifestage and personality of each of my children: the blunt, babyish toes and flat arches that support a tirelessly running body, sturdy enough to use the way a rabbit uses its hind feet in defense; the slightly larger, more graceful toes and heels that are fond of practicing "ballet," feet that often remain tucked up under a frilly skirt, feet that, when the impulse strikes, can run like the wind; the slender feet, half-child's, half-woman's, that kick off their shoes whenever they enter a room, that are alternately decorously placed in a lady-like pose or sprawled out on any and all available pieces of furniture. It is those feet that have taught me the very little I know about seeing with the eyes of love.[11]

One of the most ancient Christian perceptions is that there are traces of the divine in all of creation. If we are attuned, we can follow feet to the unique and God-given person and in the process disarm our defensiveness and combativeness.

This Christmas path to spiritual consciousness is pursued by many people. A friend says that in order to catch the Christmas spirit you must put yourself in its path. What he means is that you must seek the situations where matter is transparent to spirit. In principle, this could be any person, place or thing. But organized religions designate particular people, places and things as "repeat" mediators of the sacred. They are, as Yeats said, "transparent lamps around a spiritual flame."[12] Evelyn Underhill tells the story of a woman who had recently visited the island of Iona. When she returned, she told her gardener where she had been. "Ah! Iona is a very thin place," he said. She asked him what he meant by that. "There's very little between Iona and the Lord," he replied.[13]

The Christmas season is filled with people, times and places that have very "little between them and the Lord." We put ourselves in those situations and hope spirit will visit our sluggish flesh. We attend to midnight Mass with a choir of carols; to a gift wrapped in gold and silver that, when opened, does not contain black socks; to a tree of many ornaments with an heirloom star, a tarnished reminder that there have been others before us; to our family, heads bowed and hands held around a table of food; to a soft snow seen from inside a warm room, preferably accompanied by the crackle of logs on the fire; to houses strung with lights under a sky strung with stars; and, always, to a sleeping child—any child, sleeping anywhere. In these settings, intuition can transcend intellect and we go out of ourselves into a larger, more spacious world that for the moment seems, as we say, "real beyond belief."

Anthony de Mello tells a wonderful story about the intuition of the spiritual through the physical:

The Temple had stood on an island two miles out to sea. And it held a thousand bells. Big bells, small bells, bells fashioned by the best craftsmen in the world. When a wind blew or a storm raged, all the temple bells would peal out in unison, producing a symphony that sent the heart of the hearer into raptures.

But over the centuries the island sank into the sea and, with it, the temple and the bells. An ancient tradition said that the bells continued to peal out, ceaselessly, and could be heard by anyone who listened attentively. Inspired by this tradition, a young man traveled thousands of miles, determined to hear those bells. He sat for days on the shore, opposite the place where the temple had once stood, and listened—listened with all his heart. But all he could hear was the sound of the waves breaking on the shore. He made every effort to push away the sound of the waves so that he could hear the bells. But all to no avail; the sound of the sea seemed to flood the universe.

He kept at his task for many weeks....Finally he decided to give up the attempt....It was his final day and he went to this favourite spot to say goodbye to the sea and the sky and the wind and the coconut trees. He lay on the sands, gazing up at the sky, listening to the sound of the sea. He did not resist that sound that day. Instead, he gave himself over to it and found it was a pleasant, soothing sound, this roar of the waves. Soon he became so lost in the sound that he was barely conscious of himself, so deep was the silence that the sound produced in his heart.

In the depth of that silence, he heard it! The tinkle of a tiny bell

followed by another, and another and another…and soon every one
of the thousand temple bells was pealing out in glorious unison, and
his heart was transported with wonder and joy.[14]

Although this way of intuiting the spiritual is closely associated with Christmas, theologically it is rooted in the doctrine of creation. We do not bypass matter to attain spirit. We do not "leap-frog" creation to reach the Creator. We do not even go "through" created reality to God, leaving it behind the way a winter walker gladly discards an overcoat once inside the

The ultimate truth of

the physical world is

not found in itself, but

only in relationship to

the spiritual reality.

house. Matter and spirit, the invisible and the visible, creation and the Creator come together and, on this earth, are meant to be held together. De Mello's attached moral to his story of the temple bells has it right: "If you wish to hear the temple bells, listen to the sound of the sea."

This initial intuition of the spiritual in the physical can lead to revelation. Sometimes the tables are turned. The detective work gives way to manifestation. The one searching for the spiritual is surprised and, paradoxically, is found. The spiritual is not reluctantly tracked down; it actively comes out of hiding. As people have often said, it "bursts forth." It is then that we realize the problem was not that the spiritual was hiding but that we were blind to its presence. It was always trying to communicate with us, but in numerous ways, some conscious and some not, we avoided the encounter. Our searching was merely a way of becoming receptive. Once we open, the one who stands at the door and knocks enters. Whether intuition leads to revelation or remains intuition, our awareness is gradually altered and we come to a crucial realization. The ultimate truth of the physical world is not found in itself but only in relationship to spiritual reality.

The second way is the inner path. This path, the one less traveled, begins by turning away from the physical world, coinciding with our inner spiritual center, and then incarnating this newly realized spiritual identity in all the situations of our life. This is a complicated and dangerous road. Yet for many people it is the distinctive path that the revelation of Christmas asks us to walk:

> Where Plato declared "the true order of going" to be a mounting up by means of the beauties of earth, step by step toward the unearthly and celestial Beauty, the Christian Church—strong in her possession of the Divine paradox—compels her children to take the opposite route. She declares the true movement of the religious consciousness to be inward, not outward. It moves from the abstract and adoring sense of God Transcendent to the homely discovery of His revelation right down in the history, in the humblest surroundings and most simple and concrete ways: bringing the adoring soul from the utmost confines of thought to kneel before a poor person's baby born under the most unfortunate circumstances.[15]

The destination of this inner journey is expressed in two of the most cherished Christmas faith statements: "The Word became flesh" and "The Son of God became man."

Although in Christian faith the primary and perfect referent of the incarnational process is Jesus of Nazareth, the process itself is available in an analogous way to anyone who follows after him. As the Gospel of Luke suggests, Jesus is the "firstborn." This title relates Jesus' being to God and picks up the themes of "image of the invisible God, *firstborn* of all creatures" and the *"firstborn* of the dead" from Colossians (Col. 1:15; 1:18).[16] It also implies that God will bring others to birth in this way, and therefore they will be the spiritual brothers and sisters of Jesus. Robert Frost knows what this birth entails:

> *But God's own descent*
> *Into flesh was meant*
> *As a demonstration*
> *That the supreme merit*
> *Lay in risking spirit*
> *In substantiation.*[17]

The process of "risking spirit in substantiation" must begin with the understanding that we are spirit. Only those who know that they are the sons and daughters of God can incarnate themselves in the world, and this realization comes about only as a result of the inner journey.

William Law pointed out this inner path simply and eloquently:

> *For, though God be everywhere present, yet he is only present to thee in the deepest and most central part of thy soul. Thy natural senses cannot possess God or unite thee to him; nay, inward faculties of understanding, will and memory can only reach after God but cannot be the place of his habitation in thee. But there is a root or depth in thee from whence all these faculties come forth, as lines from a centre or as branches from the body of the tree. This depth is called the Centre, the Fund or Bottom of the soul. This depth is the unity, the eternity, I had almost said the infinity of thy soul; for it is so infinite that nothing can satisfy it or give it any rest but the infinity of God.*[18]

Spiritual consciousness is coinciding with this "root in thee," a space beyond the senses, understanding, memory and will.

Many spiritual masters suggest that getting to this "root in thee" entails a process of disidentifications.[19] We have to detach from surface allegiances in order to attach to "the Bottom of the soul." This is no easy task. We are endlessly tempted to identify ourselves with our bodies or some description of our personality or a piece of our past history or our familial or social roles. But when we look closely, we notice that we are always "a little bit more" than our bodies, personalities, past histories, and roles. We do not deny that these are aspects of the total reality we are, but we refuse to collapse our identity into any of these aspects. This "little bit more" that is always present is actually "a lot more." It is our spiritual identity as the son or daughter of God or, in Law's language, "the Centre, the Fund, the Bottom" of the soul. We must take time to coincide with this ultimate self, "to loaf and invite our soul," as Walt Whitman sang, to anchor our awareness in this transcendent realm where the divine co-constitutes our identity. "The obvious next development of personhood as transcendent of nature is the realization of the incarnation of personhood in nature," writes Beatrice Bruteau. "This is a second phase, so to speak. But it does not work out successfully, *in my opinion*, if the first phase, the realization of transcendence, has not been done thoroughly."[20] To take seriously that we are the daughters and sons of God and that this is neither privilege nor arrogance but a simple, unadorned actuality is the difficult first step of incarnation.

Once we realize our transcendent selfhood to any degree, in the provocative words of Meister Eckhart we begin to "melt." We flow into all the dimensions of our earthly life, and we infuse them with the reality we found at the Bottom of the soul, a reality infinitely more than we are yet in intimate communion with us. This flowing or manifesting dynamism is not so much a thought-out choice but the natural and spontaneous response to contact with God. Divine reality, by it nature, overflows and pours itself out. This is at least part of the meaning of the famous opening line of the Philippians hymn, "Who did not deem equality with God something to be clung to, but emptied himself..." (Phil. 2:6). Clinging and equality with God are contradictions. The divine, by definition, is diffusive of itself, not restrictive of itself. What is being reversed in this song is any understanding of God as self-enclosed, protective and aloof. It is this unconditional pouring out of life into all things that makes us stutter and stammer and finally say, "God is love":

> The whole concept of God taking on human shape, and all the liturgy and ritual around that, had simply never made any sense to me. That was because, I realized one wonderful day, it was so simple. For people with bodies, important things like love have to be embodied. That's all. God had to be embodied, or else people with bodies would never in a trillion years understand about love.[21]

The sons and daughters of the God who is love do what their Parent does —pour the love of their boundless inner persons into the physical world. his is the incarnate activity of spiritual people.

This process of incarnation may seem esoteric and beyond the reach of ordinary people. But if we pause and reflect for a moment, we realize we already know the truth of this process and already are engaged in it. We know the difference between times when we pour love into our minds and direct them at the world with compassion and times when the mind, uninformed by the love of our deeper self, goes its own way of endless analysis and cold dissection. We know the difference between times when we pour love into our desires and they become peaceful and focused and times when, uninformed by the love of our deeper self, the desires are random, chaotic, and chronically unsatisfied. We know the difference between times when our kisses are the free, spontaneous overflow of love and times when our kisses are perfunctory or greedy. In other words, we know the bliss of incarnate moments—and bliss is a tip-off to the ultimate truth about us—and we know the franticness and fear of the loveless mind, will and body. Incarnation is a theological interpretation of experiences we already cherish and hope to nurture.

The outer and inner paths are two different ways of coming to spiritual consciousness. However, they share a common conviction: the physical world is only properly appreciated from a spiritual perspective. The strange stories that surround Christmas try to get people to that perspective. They present characters, plots, motivations and settings that defy the assumptions and logic of physical consciousness. As long as we stayed locked into physical consciousness, we "don't get it." We are like the characters in John's Gospel: Nicodemus who thinks that being born again is returning to the womb; the Samaritan women who thinks that living water is found in a well; the crowds who think that eating Jesus' flesh and blood is cannibalism; Peter who thinks that letting Jesus wash him means taking a bath. The story blocks one way of thinking and opens up another. If the readers or listeners respond to the invitation, they are on a path, either outer or inner, to spiritual consciousness. On the path other strange stories will be told and spiritual consciousness will be deepened and solidified. Christ is in gestation once again.

Spiritual Seeing

As we walk the outer or inner path of spiritual consciousness, a new way of seeing emerges. We may notice things we have not noticed before. So there might be an increased capacity to take in more of what is present. But, more strikingly, we see what we have always seen but in a new way. In the Book of Revelation, Christ exclaims, "Behold! I make all things new" (Rev. 21:5). It should be stressed that he makes no new things. Rather he facilitates a way of seeing that makes all things new. People often say, "I am seeing it for the first time." What they mean is that something they have seen physically many times is now seen in a new light. This new light is the spiritual perspective. It is a light that comes from within. As e. e. cummings has written, "the eye of my eye was opened."

This spiritual perspective is called the third eye, the inner vision, and perhaps, most provocatively, the eye of the heart. St. Paul suggested that only with the "eyes of the heart enlightened" would we come to know the hope to which we are called (Eph. 1:19). The Gospels also connect seeing with the condition of the heart. It is suggested that people have eyes but do not see, ears but do not hear, and the reason is their heart has grown dull (Mt. 13:15). Conversely, when the heart is on fire the eyes are open. This idea was rooted in an ancient understanding of sight. It was thought that there was a fire in the heart that pressed upward and poured out the eyes. The eyes, to use a modern image, were like car headlights that projected beams of light. If the heart was in darkness, then the person was blind. If the heart was in light, then the person could see. As Jesus said, "The eye is the lamp of the body" (Mt. 6:22). What was presupposed was that the heart is the light of the eye.

This metaphor for spiritual perception provides a crucial insight into Luke's postresurrection story of the two disciples on the road to Emmaus (Lk. 24:13–32). When Jesus first falls in with the two disciples, their "eyes are kept from recognizing him." Jesus asks what they have been discussing as they walked along. They tell him everything about his life and death from a point of view that shows they understand none of it: "We *had* hoped that this one...." In other words, they had all the facts and even some of the "right" theological words, but they lacked spiritual vision. These blind disciples end their report to Jesus with the witness of the women who found the tomb empty, and then add, "Some of those who were with us went to the tomb and found it just as the women had said:

but him they did not see." They did not see him, just as these two disciples do not see him. Jesus' response makes it clear why: "O, foolish men and slow of heart to believe." There is a slowness in their heart, a sluggishness in their spiritual vision that is making them foolish rather than wise. They see his suffering and death only from the vantage point of physical consciousness. Although they have all the correct information, all they see is failure and ending.

Jesus tells them otherwise. He interprets the Scriptures to them so that suffering and glory are joined rather than separated. In doing this, he enables a new perspective on what they already know. As they near the village, Jesus makes to go on, but they ask him to stay. This is crucial. They are pursuing the enlightenment Jesus is offering them. "When Jesus was at table with them, he took the bread and blessed and broke it, and gave it to them. And their eyes were opened." They finally saw that blessing, breaking and giving was the key to Jesus' life and death and the key to his resurrected presence. It is at this point in the story that they give us the reason for their spiritual vision: "Did not our hearts burn within us on the road as he opened to us the Scriptures?" When the fire in the heart is lit, the inner eye sees. This is the move from physical to spiritual consciousness. It should be noted that this move takes place without abandoning the data of physical consciousness.

When the fire

in the heart is lit,

the inner eye sees.

All the spiritual stories of Christmas want to move us to the level of the heart and allow us to see all things from that perspective. This is the undying attraction of Christmas. For all our ambivalent feelings and well-aimed criticisms, Christmas gives us the gift we want but dare not ask for. Chesterton tells us what it is:

[Christmas] is rather something that surprises us from behind, from the hidden and personal part of our being; like that which can sometimes take us off our guard in the pathos of small objects or the blind pieties of the poor. It is rather as if a man had found an inner room in the very heart of his own house, which he had never suspected, and seen a light from within. It is as if he found something at the back of his own heart that betrayed him into good.[22]

Christmas is celebrated in the unsuspected inner room at the back of the heart where we are betrayed into good. It is in this inner sanctum that the Christ child is born and to this inner sanctum that the spiritual stories try to bring us.

Three Circles of Christmas Stories

It is helpful to organize the spiritual stories of Christmas in three expanding circles. In the first, inner circle are the primary stories, the infancy narratives of Matthew and Luke. It is these stories that inspire all the other Christmas stories. Even though we may be lulled into unquestioning acceptance by hearing them so frequently, they are filled with events that physical consciousness cannot comprehend. We are often encouraged to hear the message of Christmas but seldom counselled to maintain the strangeness of the biblical stories. Yet the revelation is in the strangeness, and the stories themselves ready the reader for the impact by telling us to "Behold!" "Behold, you will be reduced to silence…" (Lk. 1:20); "Behold, you will conceive…" (Lk. 1:31); "Behold, wise men from the East came to Jerusalem…" (Mt. 2:1); "Behold, an angel of the Lord appeared to Joseph in a dream…" (Mt. 2:13, 19); "Behold, the star they had seen at its rising went before them…" (Mt. 2:9); "Behold, the virgin shall be with child…" (Mt. 1:23); "Behold, I announce to you good news of great joy which will be for all the people…" (Lk. 2:10). This injunction to behold is an invitation to ponder, to prolong perception until spiritual sight arises. This is the path of Mary who "kept all these things, pondering them in her heart" (Lk. 2:19).

Yet this strangeness we are asked to behold until it changes our way of seeing is often successfully ignored. The dark drive of fear may be the hidden reason we avoid the call to spiritual consciousness. As Peter Occhiogrosso has written, "I have come to realize that spiritual awareness, when seriously engaged, is something that cannot but be upsetting."[23] We can never underestimate the lengths to which we will go not to be upset. However, it may just be a matter of selective attention. When we approach the stories with overriding historical and theological questions, we tend to get historical and theological considerations.

Historical questions about the birth of Christ seem to work on two levels. On the first and most heated level, there has been and continues to be much discussion on whether the events narrated ever happened. Was there a census of Caesar Augustus? Was Jesus born in Bethlehem? Was his birth visited by Magi from the East and did they have a consultation with Herod? Was there a real traveling star and through astronomical calculation can we pin down the exact year of its appearance? Did shepherds visit the birth? Was there a slaughter of the innocents? Did Mary visit Elizabeth? Was Jesus virginally conceived? Etc. In other words, do the episodes in the infancy narratives reflect, in a literal manner, events in history?

A second level of historical concern tries to reconstruct the issues behind the stories. The focus is not on a precise match between text and event but on a general correlation between what was happening in the Christian community and the way the infancy stories are told. Is the emphasis on the virginal conception of Jesus an attempt to respond to allegations that Jesus was illegitimate? Is the arrival of the Magi a symbolic way of saying the church was making converts in the Gentile world? Does the saying "no room in the inn" refer to the rejection of Jesus by Israel's religious leaders? Is the flight to and return from Egypt meant to reflect an early church position that Jesus had recapitulated and gone beyond the Mosaic covenant? Does the prominent place of John the Baptist in the Lucan story signal an unbreakable connection with *true* priestly, prophetic and apocalyptic traditions of Israel? Etc. In other words, what concerns and perceptions of the early Christian community are embodied in the imaginative constructions of the infancy narratives?

The answers to these questions are exceedingly complex, and even the way of phrasing the questions is open to debate. There are books that carefully and passionately argue one position or another. These concerns often monopolize discussions about the infancy narratives. They have a very important role to play in exploring the relationship between myth and history in the Christian tradition. Yet the energy of this investigation tends to push the texts farther and farther into the past, into the difficult-to-trace origins of Christian history. The result, intended or not, is that the infancy narratives are kept at arm's length. Whether we defend or debunk the factuality of the stories or argue one interpretation over another, we are still concerned, initially and all too often endlessly, with the past, the world *behind* the text. In our approach here, the emphasis will be on the consciousness of contemporary readers as they encounter the story. The focus is on the world *in front of* the text. The question of strangeness is not in what happened then but in what is happening now.

Approaching the stories with overriding theological concerns can also contribute to avoiding the strangeness that is meant to jolt us into spiritual consciousness. The infancy narratives have generated many theological debates, but the dominant theological declaration that Christian tradition has attached to Christmas is, "God becomes man." For sophisticated minds this phrasing may be unnuanced in the extreme, but it is a "sticking point" for both unbelievers and believers. Sigrid Undset parodies the unbeliever's caution:

Yes, in that way—whispers the chilly, cautious person of the present day—in that way we also can join you in the stable. If the little Boy in the crib is a symbol of the longing in each one of us for something beyond the bounds of sense, of our presentiments of immortality, then we also can remain with the shepherds in the stable. We can worship Mary's child, we moderns, as a symbol or as a type, as the great Teacher, a genius, a superman. But as God in Man? "Genuisti eum qui te fecit?" Mary, could you have brought forth Him who created you? Can you expect us to believe this sort of thing in the twentieth?[24]

Physical consciousness has stumbled upon a theological truth that it cannot fit into its world.[25] The strangeness of it has been acknowledged, but it has also been dismissed. This is to be expected. Theological truths do not emerge out of physical consciousness. They are grounded in spiritual perceptions, and without this grounding they are confusing and misleading. Sigrid Undset has hit on the perfect phrasing of this confusion. It is the incredulity of people who are locked into physical consciousness and yet forced to comment on the articulations of spiritual consciousness. What is seemingly being proposed for belief is so far outside the boundaries of their mind that they are affronted by the very prospect of acceptance. "Can you expect us…?" The response is no, not in your present state of awareness.

However, there has been another quite prevalent response to the unbeliever's discombobulation. Believers counterpunch. They insist that this is the case: Mary did indeed give birth to the one who created her. This truth is revealed by God in inspired Scriptures, backed up by dogmatic degrees, and reenforced by centuries of nuanced theological argumentation. Added to these powerful reenforcements is the assurance that we are dealing with a mystery that can never be fully understood. It calls for an act of faith and only afterward a tentative and partial inquiry of mind, an inquiry that can illuminate but never refute the revealed truth. In one sense all of this is proper procedure. It is placing the theological truth of Christmas in its rightful collective context of community and tradition. But it is a highly formal approach that keeps the focus off the content of the truth and on the external factors that bolster belief — revealed in Scripture, defined by church, and theologically defended. The prestige of the tradition muscles the mind into an assent, "O, yes, the child is God."

If this happens, the unbeliever and the believer find themselves in very similar positions. The unbeliever dismissed the truth too quickly, and so it did not lead him into spiritual vision. The believer accepted the truth too quickly, and so it did not lead her into spiritual vision. One will not let the strangeness in, and the other lets the strangeness in without pondering it. "Mary gave birth to the one who created her" is truly a strange statement. It is part of the spiritual rhetoric of Christmas and can be the catalyst that shifts physical consciousness to a wider perspective. A powerful truth of Christmas is encoded in these symbolic words, but we can tame them and make them useless by both mindless rejection and mindless acceptance.

There is another approach. Eknath Easwaran's remarks on the true battlefield of the Hindu classic the *Bhagavad Gita* start us in the right direction:

> *Once I was on a train going from Delhi to Simla, high on the Himalayas, and on the way we passed through Kurukshetra, the historical battlefield of the Bhagavad Gita. My fellow passengers were talking about the tremendous battle which took place there, and when we arrived at the scene they eagerly climbed out to have a look. To me there was no need to disembark, because I already had an inkling that the real battlefield of the Gita was right inside each passenger on the train.*[26]

The infancy narratives are maps to inner reality, and to find "the place where Christ was born" we do not have to journey to Bethlehem and "climb out to have a look." What we have to do is take the map and go "right inside." The stories are finely crafted literary expressions of the spiritual reality that came to birth in the whole life, death and resurrection of Jesus Christ. They will take us into that reality and expose every detour and dead-end until we finally arrive at "the child wrapped in swaddling clothes and laid in a manger."

This is a literary-spiritual approach to the infancy narratives. It wagers that if we treat them as mythic expressions of interior spiritual journeys, there will be a major payoff. Since the Gospels are an amalgam of many different forms—history, theology, spiritual teaching, myth, prophetic denunciation, etc., no one approach is adequate to interpret the whole. In fact, not even every passage of the infancy narratives is amenable to a spiritual-literary interpretation. But much of the Gospel in general and many of the passages and episodes of the infancy narratives come to life when we read them with spiritual-literary glasses. In this reading something happens that does not often happen in historical-theological readings. What exactly that is will be revealed in the course of this book. But a personal witness to it is found at the end of Cullen Murphy's article "Who Do Men Say That I Am." This *Atlantic Monthly* article is a reportorial piece about all the historical and theological rethinking of Jesus of Nazareth that is going on in contemporary scholarship. For anyone interested in spiritual-literary approaches (and who also happens to be a Chicagoan) the last paragraph is more than a "good closer":

> There is something to be said, finally, for mythology. Around
> Christmastime last year the context I found myself in was Chicago,
> Illinois. I had spent a long day talking with various scholars about
> Jesus research, and at times I had had the distinct impression of being

present at some sort of clinical procedure. Walking up Michigan Avenue in the early evening through a light snowfall, I came to the Water Tower, brightly lit. On the pavement nearby was a Salvation Army band, which, as I approached, began to play "O Little Town of Bethlehem." And I must say that it was quite a thrill.[27]

When was the last time Christmas thrilled us?

Using a spiritual-literary approach does not mean we will neglect history and theology. Although the "child wrapped in swaddling clothes and laid in a manger" does not refer *only* to one person of past history, the map to the child's presence is a historical document. So we will consider some of the historical questions around the infancy narratives. They will not, however, preoccupy us or be the scales on which we weigh the relevance of Christmas. We will also consider the theological truths of Christmas, but not as highly polished statements of abstract reasoning. They represent the conclusions and outcomes of spiritual journeys. They will come alive for us only if we know and, in some way, experience for ourselves the spiritual path that leads to them. Our reflections, therefore, primarily will be in the poetic and mystical traditions of the spiritual masters.[28] When it is appropriate, we will tie in the hedged calculations of the historian and the second-order considerations of the theologian.

The infancy narratives are the primary stories of Christmas, but they are not the only ones with spiritual intent. In the second, middle circle are stories that imaginatively recast the primary stories. In the course of Christian history there has grown up around the brief prologues of Matthew and Luke a host of secondary stories. These stories play upon the details of the infancy stories or supply what is missing. T. S. Eliot's *The Journey of the Magi*, W. H. Auden's *For the Time Being*, Clive Barnes's *The Innkeeper's Wife*, Gian Carlo Mennoti's *Amahl and the Night Visitors*, and Henry Van Dyke's *The Other Wise Man* fit into this circle. At their best, these stories express and communicate the spiritual perceptions that are indebted to the primary stories. In other words, these stories are part of a trajectory, a tradition that takes its inspiration from the original scriptural narratives.

Of course, not all of these secondary stories are in this spiritual tradition. Although they borrow material from Matthew and Luke, they go their own way. They become adventures in physical consciousness, not provokers of spiritual awareness. Matthew's Joseph is developed into an angry cuckold set straight by an angelic dream. Luke's Mary is a timid young girl, frightened and confused by what is happening but assured by an older woman. These are fascinating story-lines and often highly entertaining, but they are not about the business of engendering spiritual sensitivity. Therefore, there is a need to discern which stories should be told side by side with the biblical texts as genuine companions on the journey of the spirit.

An illumined guide can show us the spiritual meaning of even the most common and hackneyed of Christmas stories.

In the third, outer circle are all the other countless stories that surround Christmas. O. Henry's *The Gift of the Magi*, Dickens's *A Christmas Carol*, Hans Christian Andersen's *The Fir Tree*, Clement Moore's *'Twas the Night Before Christmas*, Dylan Thomas's *A Child's Christmas in Wales*, Dr. Suess's *How the Grinch Stole Christmas*, and "How

St. Francis Taught the People of Gubbio to Feed Their Wolf" are a few of the stories in this crowded circle. Once again, not all these stories that cluster around Christmas serve the spirit of Christmas. Many are tales

of nostalgia and sentiment. Others appear to be ordinary efforts, but to the eye and ear of the spiritually sensitive they are creative and brilliant encouragements to spiritual consciousness. An illumined guide can show us the spiritual meaning of even the most common and hackneyed of Christmas stories. Listen to that troubadour of Christmas, G. K. Chesterton, uncover the spiritual center of the Santa Claus story:

> *What has happened to me has been the very reverse of what appears to be the experience of most of my friends. Instead of dwindling to a point, Santa Claus has grown larger and larger in my life until he fills almost the whole of it. It happened in this way. As a child I was faced with a phenomenon requiring explanation. I hung up at the end of my bed an empty stocking, which in the morning became a full stocking. I had done nothing to produce the things that filled it. I had not worked for them, or made them or helped to make them. I had not even been good — far from it. And the explanation was that a certain being whom people called Santa Claus was benevolently disposed toward me. Of course, most people who talk about these things get into a state of some mental confusion by attaching tremendous importance to the name of the entity. We called him Santa Claus, because everyone called him Santa Claus; but the name of a god is a mere human label. His real name may have been Williams. It may have been the Archangel Uriel. What we believed was that a certain benevolent agency did give us those toys for nothing. And, as I say, I believe it still. I have merely extended the idea. Then I only wondered who put the toys in the stocking; now I wonder who put the stocking by the bed, and the bed in the room, and the room in the house, and the house on the planet, and the great planet in the void. Once I only thanked Santa Claus for a few dolls and crackers, now, I thank him for stars and street faces and wine and the great sea. Once I thought*

it delightful and astonishing to find a present so big that it only went halfway into the stocking. Now I am delighted and astonished every morning to find a present so big that it takes two stockings to hold it, and then leaves a great deal outside; it is the large and preposterous present of myself, as to the origin of which I can offer no suggestion except that Santa Claus gave it to me in a fit of peculiarly fantastic goodwill.[29]

What Chesterton, the guide, has shown is that Santa Claus is a contemporary embodiment of grace, a spiritual perception that runs throughout Luke's account of the birth of Christ. The story of Santa Claus, for those who know how to see, is a companion on the journey of the spirit.

Spiritual Guides

My grandmother played the concertina. The dictionary defines concertina as a "small, hexagonal accordion with bellows, and buttons for keys." If it was a family heirloom, passed on from mother to daughter, and crushed in a packed bag that traveled from Dublin to New York, the definition would include leather straps on each side worn from handholding, steel ribs bent from the rigors of push and pull, and both broken and unbudgeable buttons. It made for richer music.

The concertina sat lifeless on a chair in my grandmother's living room. It was scrunched up, enfolded, its inner structure hidden from sight. Then my grandmother would pick up this dead thing and sit in the chair herself, the concertina on her lap. Her hands at home inside the leather straps, her arms would push and pull. The spine of the instrument was suddenly revealed, breath blew through it, and music stopped every conversation. It was not Mozart. But I swear, even the lame tapped a foot.

So it is with the strange stories of Christmas, especially in the first circle of Scripture. They are inheritances from the past; their power lies hidden and compressed. They sit lifeless until someone knows how to tell and interpret them. They need to be pushed and pulled until their spine is revealed and the music heard. Unfortunately, my grandmother is not available. But others are.

On a busy corner near where I live, a blind woman could not go forward. Her seeing eye dog had steered her up against a bus-stop bench and continued to nudge her against it. Every time she tried to push ahead, she just pushed against the bench. Finally, she called out, "Is there anybody there who can see." A man instantly and explosively responded, "I can, sister, I can." He helped her. If we wish to go forward, there are times when we need somebody who can see better than we can.

This is one of the blessings of belonging to a community and a tradition. One person's blindness is complemented by another's sight. There are people who know the secret at the center of the story, women and men for whom the strangeness is familiar. They have already traveled the territory we are only beginning to explore. They see more fully than we do, and they will show us the shock of the story slowly. Our eyes need time to become accustomed to the light. Also, they know how others have understood the story and the basic vision of the people who created, preserved, and continue to interpret the story. Most importantly, they are personally acquainted with the mystery that the story humbly tries to express and communicate. Therefore, they never turn the story into an idol. It is merely a gate they open so we may go inside. The tradition of spiritual stories is preserved within a community of spiritual guides.

Many of our guides will be spiritual luminaries—Chrysostom, Augustine, Bernard, Eckhart, Francis, Merton, Bruteau, scholars, saints and mystics. Some will be toilers and trudgers (like most of us) who for a moment saw a light. All will be people who have intuited the heart of the biblical story and learned to discern its influence through the developing traditions of Christmas. We will take help from them and from wherever we can get it.

However, there is one less-than-luminous guide, and he is typing this sentence. The Matthean Jesus warned against the blind leading the blind (Mt. 15:14). I do not suspect this to be the case—mostly because when I have talked to you in church and in class, in conferences and in workshops, and have said some of these ideas, you have not shook your head no but simply lifted your hand, palm down, and wiggled it side to side. I take that to be an affirmative maybe and move away from the strong verdict of blind guide to the milder judgment of blurred guide.

Once Jesus touched a man's eyes and asked him what he saw. He replied, "I see people but they look like walking trees" (Mk. 8:24). Jesus touched him again and the man saw clearly. If you are between the first and second touch of Jesus, you are a blurred guide. You know something is there and you can almost see it. That is how I evaluate my spiritual role—a blurred, never to be clear-eyed, guide. I can only glimpse the spiritual forms of Christmas, and so I present them with an accompanying Christmas mist. On the concertina I play a wildly off-key but recognizable rendition of "O Come, All Ye Faithful."

Chapter 3

Waking Up on Christmas Morning

Adam and Eve woke up. They were hungry and thirsty.

Later, on reflection, they did not know if they woke up and were hungry and thirsty, or if hunger and thirst had awakened them.

But they ate and drank, and they were full. It was good.

Six hours later they were hungry and thirsty again.

They said to one another, "We must not have done it right."

So they ate and drank very carefully, savoring every sip and chewing every bite, and they were full. It was good.

Six hours later they were hungry and thirsty again.

So a third time they ate and drank, taking even greater care in chewing and sipping. It was good.

Six hours later they were hungry and thirsty again.

Then it dawned on them. That is the way it was going to be. Hungry and thirsty, then eating and drinking. Then once again, hungry and thirsty, then eating and drinking. Then once again....

It was not enough.

They shouted out their frustration. "What are we? Asses tethered to a feeding trough? Oxen tied to a manger?"

God heard this shout and took their protest as a prayer. He sent an angel named Gariel to a town named Nazareth to a virgin named Mary.

Gabriel said, "Adam and Eve hunger and thirst and you must prepare a feast."

Mary spread herself like a linen tablecloth on the earth and the Son of the Most High was born. Shepherds attended his birth and found new flocks to tell what they had seen and heard.

One day they came upon Adam and Eve roaming around outside the garden. The shepherds knew that what they had to say Adam and Eve wanted to hear: "We bring you glad tidings of great joy meant for all the people. There has been born to you a child, the Messiah and the Lord. Go to Bethlehem and you will find a child wrapped in swaddling clothes and laid in a manger."

Adam and Eve were not sure of all that the invitation entailed, but they decided they needed some direction to their roaming. They set out for Bethlehem, the house of Bread. When they arrived at the birth, they were surprised to see an ox and an ass grazing around the manger. As they walked past them, Adam and Eve nodded. Did they know these beasts? Then they looked down at the child wrapped in swaddling clothes and laid in a manger. Before long they knelt.

Mary took the hand of Eve and placed it on the chest of the child, over his heart. The eyes of the child opened and Eve drank from his eyes.

Then Mary took the hand of Adam and placed it on the chest of the child, over his heart. The mouth of the child opened and Adam ate from the mouth of the child.

Then Adam and Eve spoke as one: "We tie ourselves to this manger."

I have told this story in both large and small groups. It does not have the same impact as "How St. Francis Taught the People of Gubbio to Feed Their Wolf." It causes more puzzlement than illumination. People quickly grasp the formal plot of the story—Adam and Eve's problem is solved by the Christ child. But what the problem is and how Christ is a solution is difficult to determine. The story is cryptic in the extreme, and it demands a knowledge of biblical themes in order to catch the multiple associations. It wants to inculcate a spiritual consciousness—most stories with God as a character have this ambition. Yet there is a definite need for a guide—blind, blurred or sighted—to take the story apart, play with the images, comment on the associations, run with the insights, and in general tease us into seeing ourselves in a new way.

Adam and Eve

In the story and in biblical mythology Adam and Eve are not two distinct characters but *the* man and *the* woman. They represent the perennial human situation, and what they undergo is in principle available to everyone. This suggests a different and more diverse gathering around the manger than is usually envisioned. If Adam and Eve show up at the birth of Christ, the implication is that no one is excluded.

This is certainly the case with one creche scene I visit. Everyone seems to show up in figurine—Buddha, Krishna, a Vietnamese refugee, a farm worker, two young lovers, carolers, a man in a nightshirt with a light (what could he be looking for?). I understand that any figurine you bring joins the assembled throng. This contemporary crew of planet earth has precedent. In popular lore, Matthew's Magi and Luke's shepherds join one another to symbolize both ends of the human spectrum. The rich Magi and the poor shepherds, the wise Magi and the simple shepherds, the bold Magi and the timid shepherds, etc. However we conceive them, they are meant as bookends. Between them, this story suggests, is Adam and Eve, that is, the entire human race.

The birth of Christ is the special celebration of the Christian peoples, but in a characteristic act of generosity its blessings are meant for all women and men. It is not meant for all people in the sense that they should become Christian. Expanding the membership of the Christian churches is not the same as being fed by the child. Neither is it meant for these people in the sense that if they do not "come to the manger" they will find neither God nor themselves. Arguing the exclusivity or uniqueness or superiority of Christ is not the same as saying this child fulfills a universal human promise. The birth of Christ is meant for all in the sense that the Christian revelation responds to an unavoidable human question, a search that arises wherever men and women wake up.

Of course, the search of awakened men and women may also lead them to Buddha or Mohammed or Krishna or Moses. We take help from wherever we can get it. We do not have to be an adherent of a religion to benefit from its revelation. We do not have to be a Taoist to learn from the *Tao Te Ching* or a Hindu to learn from the *Bhagavad Gita* or a Moslem to learn from the *Koran* or a Buddhist to learn from the *Dhammapada* or a Christian to learn from the Gospel of Luke. All we have to be is open. For the spiritual searcher the religions of the world are meant for the people of the world. As diverse as they are, as in need of criticism as they are, as in need of dialogue with one another as they are—they represent a cosmic revelation, "a ray of the truth which enlightens all human beings."[1] Therefore, all are invited to the birth of Christ and an angel in the night sky, even after he has calmed you down, is difficult to refuse: "I bring you glad tidings of great joy which is meant for *all* the people" (Lk. 2:10).[2]

An angel in the night sky, even after he has calmed you down, is difficult to refuse.

Waking Up Hungry and Thirsty

The first line of the story tells the tale—Adam and Eve wake up. "Waking up" is one of many metaphors for the process of "coming to spiritual consciousness." The metaphors are usually paired to bring out the "before and after" nature of this perceptual change. One who is asleep wakes up; one who is dead comes to life; one who is blind sees; one who is lost is found; one who once walked in the flesh now walks in the spirit. Each of these metaphors has its own distinctive slant on the process of coming to spiritual consciousness. If they were pursued seriously, they would take the seeker through a slightly different set of experiences and reflections. Yet they all point to the same event and emphasize that it is a positive repositioning of the human person in relationship to the mystery of life and death.

One weakness of these metaphors is that they may give the impression that this consciousness shift happens in a moment. Perhaps for some people that is the case. Certainly there are breakthrough experiences that undergird any new structure of awareness. However, there is a major difference between a moment of illumination and a consciousness that is permanently enlightened.[3] Rather than speak of a shift to spiritual consciousness as an event, it is probably more accurate to speak of it as a process that includes many different experiences—valleys, peaks and plateaus. Charles Tart talks about the process of waking up as a "continuum of enlightenment" in which there are some crucial "jumps."[4] I would add that there are many setbacks and falls. The dominance of physical consciousness does not easily yield. In this sense, the waking up of Adam and Eve is not the prelude to what happens but a title that tells what the story is all about. Everything they do, say and undergo is part of a "journey of awakening."

This journey begins with two awakenings: Adam and Eve open their eyes together. It does not begin with one (man) from which another emerges (wo-man). There is mutuality from the start. We are not islanded individuals who must then reach across a distance to another island. We are essentially relational. Community, not individuality, is our natural condition. This insight bypasses the primacy of Adam in the second creation story of Genesis and develops the provocative verse of Genesis 1:37: "So God created humankind in the divine image / In the image of God, God created them / Male and Female, God created them." God creates community because, as later Christian theology will assert, God is community.

This mutuality is the essential structure of human existence. Although we continually talk about the dignity of the person, the more fundamental category is plural. We always exist as persons. From the moment of conception, who we are includes who we came from and who we are with. The umbilical cord may be cut at birth, but we continue to carry and develop an inherited genetic package. Also we enter into a field of family dynamics that eventually widens into neighborhood, school, family of choice, work, and societal relationships. Our uniqueness emerges and stays within these relational patterns. From the point of view of both nature and nurture, no one—no matter how strongly we may feel it at any given time—is alone. We exist as a web of relationships.

Adam and Eve's shared awakening is closely tied to their shared experience of hunger and thirst. In fact, they are so intertwined that Adam and Eve cannot tell whether their awakening preceded their hunger and thirst or whether their hunger and thirst caused them to wake up. This hunger and thirst naturally leads to eating and drinking, and the pattern of physical existence is established. We live in a recurring rhythm of need and fulfillment. The story, mimicking Genesis, states that this rhythm is good. In a no-nonsense, almost chastising way, Thomas Merton reminds us what is good about it:

> From the moment you put a piece of bread in your mouth you are part of the world.... Who made the bread? Where did it come from? You are in relationship to the guy who made this stuff. And what is your relationship to him? Do you deserve to be eating this stuff...do you have a right to it? That is the world and that is no illusion.[5]

What is good about hunger-thirst / eating-drinking is that it wakes us up out of the illusion of separateness into the real, interdependent world.

This interdependent world goes beyond the human community. Human existence characterized by hunger-thirst / eating-drinking is not self-enclosed. It is essentially open to and dependent on the earth. We do not have the resources to survive within our own skin boundaries. In fact, the ongoing activity of eating and drinking makes it difficult to determine where we let off and where other creatures begin:

> *Eating is an intimate relationship. We place pieces of external reality inside ourselves; we swallow them more deeply inside, where they are incorporated into our own stuff, our own bodily being of flesh and blood. It is a remarkable fact that we turn parts of external reality into our own substance. We are least separate from the world in eating. The world enters into us; it becomes us. We are constituted by portions of the world.*[6]

Hunger and thirst are the fiercest of human needs, but eating and drinking are too narrowly understood if they stay egocentrically focused on human fulfillment. They can widen our awareness and regain for us the easily forgotten truth of our kinship and dependency on the earth. Eating and drinking are acts of intimacy and communion so complete and pervasive that they often escape our notice: "We are constituted by portions of the world."

Christmas can contribute to this widening of awareness. It is a feast that not only notices the interdependency of people and the earth but celebrates it. It reveals that the connectedness of all things is not a brute fact but an incredibly beautiful design. The customs of Christmas want to plunge us into this design and encourage us to delight in it. Christmas dinner is not about fueling the furnace. It is a meal to be eaten with awareness, an awareness that brings powerful emotions: "the world as a nurturative place; oneself as worthy of receiving such nurturance, excitement, primal contact with the nurturative mother; the security of being at home in the world, connection to other life forms, thankfulness too—the religious will add—for the fruits of creation."[7] Christmas, with all its special foods, hopes to solicit these perceptions so that we can bless the hunger-thirst/eating-drinking pattern of our lives. For all the pain it sometimes causes us and for the consternation it often throws us into, our dependent physical existence is good. Are you hungry and thirsty? Bless and pass the food.

The real genius of Christmas, however, is the multiple ways it reenforces the vision of human interdependency. It stresses again and again that waking up means waking up together. A recurring theme of the feasts, stories and songs of Christmas is reconciliation. The alienated and the estranged are united. No one developed this theme more thoroughly than Charles Dickens, who turned every lonely "Bah, humbug!" into a communitarian "God bless us, every one." At no time of the year was restraint Dickens' strength, but at the sight of the "affectionate attachment" of Christmas his words tumbled, one after the other, like toys from Santa's sack.

Who can be insensible to the outpourings of good feeling, and the honest interchange of affectionate attachment which abound at this season of the year. A Christmas family party! We know nothing in nature more delightful! There seems a magic in the very name of Christmas. Petty jealousies and discords are forgotten; social feelings are awakened, in bosoms to which they have long been strangers; father and son, or brother and sister, who have met and passed with averted gaze, or a look of cold recognition, for months before, proffer and return the cordial embrace, and bury their past animosities in their present happiness. Kindly hearts that have yearned toward each other but have been withheld by false notions of pride and self-dignity are again reunited, and all is kindness and benevolence! Would that Christmas lasted the whole year through (as it ought) and that the prejudices and passions which deform our better nature were never called into action among those to whom they should ever be strangers![8]

For all the rhetorical overkill, Dickens is praising Christmas for overcoming what "deforms our better nature" and brings us together. Dickens does not explore exactly what the "magic in the very name of Christmas" is that performs this feat. In the story, Adam and Eve eventually learn what the "magic" is by meeting the "magician."

Dickens focused on the family, but the Christmas call to relationality goes beyond family. The cardinal takes off his robes, puts on an apron, and waits table at the Center for the Homeless. Strangers are welcome, the poor are fed, every child has a toy. Political leaders plead for peace. In the Slavonic churches, at the end of Christmas Mass, the people kiss one another on both cheeks and say, "Christ is born." The response is, "Truly he is born," and the kisses are repeated. *This goes on until everyone in the church has been kissed by everyone else.* This may take a little time, but there is no doubt in people's mind that this is the appropriate action to celebrate Christmas.

Even the world of war, the world of extreme and violent separateness, has been known to be affected by the Christmas vision. There is a moment from World War I that is almost too sentimental to recall, a story that when it is over, you have to say, "It actually happened." It is often called the Christmas miracle of World War I.[9]

The "guns of August" boomed in 1914 and threw Europe into war. In November Pope Benedict XV called for a cease-fire on Christmas day. The response of both sides was, "Impossible." The German High Command told their troops "to let their hearts beat to God during the coming season and to keep their fists on the enemy. This is a military expression of the classic split between spirit and flesh, a split that the feast of Christmas struggles to overcome.

However, the generals were not heard and on sundown of Christmas eve the firing stopped. Troops on both sides came out of the trenches. They sang carols and exchanged gifts. On Christmas day they ate together and played soccer games. As evening fell, they embraced one another and said goodbye. Christmas was over.

The next day was war as usual. It was a one-time event; it never happened again.

A young English soldier wrote home that the Germans were friendly, "jolly good fellows." At the end of his letter he stated simply the conundrum of that Christmas truce: "Both sides have started firing and are enemies again. Strange it all seems, doesn't it?"

Strange it all seems, doesn't it? This strangeness is a path to the Christmas revelation. What is strange is that for a moment he glimpsed the brotherhood of himself and the enemy, the common bondedness beneath the surface disparity. In the next moment that vision was gone and the perception of angry isolation and violence took its place. When this happens, this rapid alternation of opposing visions, we become confused. Which vision is truthful? Which way of seeing and behaving reflects the deepest reality of our situation? If we opt for the vision of communion, we will be at odds with the majority and become as strange as a Christmas truce. If we opt for the vision of separateness, we can explain the glimpse of communion as a freak occurrence—battle stress. Then we can go about the acceptable business of protecting ourselves. Waking up does not preclude going back to sleep.

However, the sense of communion, which we saw for a moment,

is not easily dismissed. It exercises a pull, an attraction, a fascination. This is not the lure of an ideal, a pious wish that things were different, or a child's tantrum that things are not the way they should be. What is nagging at us is the pull of actuality. The metaphysical truth is that we are all interdependent realities; the existential fact is that we are estranged from this communion. Communion is who we are, but we are not who we really are. We are out of touch with ourselves. Therefore, Christmas is not one day of naiveté and idealism in a year of unrelenting realism. Christmas is the day of the real in a year of illusion. If we wake up on Christmas morning, we may realize we have been sleepwalking the rest of the year.

This moment in the journey of awakening is often called "horizontal solidarity." We realize a mutual relatedness with all creation, and hot on the heels of this realization is the simple yet profound evaluation that it is good. Yet somehow it is not enough. We cry out in frustration and question our identity: "What are we? Asses tethered to a feeding trough? Oxen tied to a manger?" It seems unfair that having awakened out of separateness into a world of communion we now become as restless in that interdependency as we were in our previous isolation. The journey continues.

Getting to God

It came to pass one Christmas that a family was gathered for dinner. On the table was a turkey and all the trimmings. It was a tradition for each member of the family to say something before the feasting began and so contribute to a group grace. Around the table it went, each member of the family giving thanks for one thing or another until it came to the youngest, who was a five-year-old boy.

He began by thanking the turkey which, although he had not yet tasted it, he was sure would be good. This was a novel piece of gratitude, and he followed it with more predictable credits given to his mother for cooking the turkey and his father for buying it. Then he began a chain of thank-yous, surfacing hidden benefactors and linking them together. "And the checker at the Jewel, and all the Jewel people, and the farmers who feed the turkeys to get them fat, and the people who make the feed, and the people who bring the turkeys to the store...." His little Colombo mind was playing detective, tracing the path of the turkey to his plate. This litany went on for some time and ended with, "Did I miss anyone?"

"God," said his older brother.

"I was just getting to him," the child solemnly said, unflustered.

This five-year-old boy is a budding contemporary theologian. His reflections embody an anthropological approach to God. He starts with a dimension of human experience—the interlocking food chain — and eventually arrives at God as the ultimate support and direction of this endeavor that he has so carefully expounded. Other contemporary theologians agree with his approach. Karl Rahner sees the question of God as emerging out of the question of the human. "The question of God...must be posed as the question of the supporting ground, the origin, and the future of the question that we ourselves are."[10] Thomas Merton considers it a paradox: "Our knowledge of God is paradoxically a knowledge not of Him as the object of our scrutiny but of ourselves as utterly dependent on His saving and merciful knowledge."[11] John Updike, the novelist, gives the same insight a much-needed affective expression: "God is a bottomless encouragement to our faltering and frightened being."[12] This approach explores human experiences—trust, questioning, intimacy, finitude, love, compassionate action, the quest for justice, etc. —until the supporting ground, the merciful dependency, the bottomless encouragement comes into view. Dig in the soil of the human long enough and you will find the bedrock of God.

In the story of the waking up of Adam and Eve the springboard experience into the awareness of God is a particular pattern of perception that often accompanies Christmas. The delights of the physical world are tasted and relished and praised as good, yet the needs they fill return again and again. There is nothing wrong with this, but there is something in us that rebels at repetition and tedium. We are not fully accounted for. Eating and drinking does not calm our restlessness. A new hunger and thirst develops, one that even the choicest cuts and finest vintages cannot assuage. We are not clear about what it is and not sure where it comes from. It is not a lack in the physical world. The physical world is meeting all our physical needs. Yet if eating and drinking, eating and drinking, eating and drinking is all we are, we raise our voices in protest and puzzlement: "What is a man / If the chief good and market of his time / but be to sleep and feed: a beast, no more."[13]

What is it about us that cannot be exhausted in the recurrent patterns of physical existence?

The restlessness stems from a surplus in us; and when we realize this, our consciousness changes from "horizontal solidarity" with the earth and our fellow creatures to a "vertical quest." What is it about us that cannot be exhausted in the recurrent patterns of physical existence?

This experience of dissatisfaction often accompanies Christmas consumerism:

Last Christmastime I sat in a cafe inside a fashionable department store, watching the shoppers come and go. Most of them, I thought, had not come to buy things they already wanted. It was as if they had come looking for something to want—something that might fill a nameless need, even if only for a moment.... To me, it is a comment on the nobility of human nature that even in the midst of such a smorgasbord of things and activities and sensations, we still feel a need for something real.... Even today, with the abundance within reach for more people than ever, we need something more than the physical world can offer.[14]

We are often driven by a "nameless need," searching the material world for "something we know not what." We collect things, activities and sensations, but *this* hunger and thirst cannot be filled by multiplying possessions and experiences. We are searching in the wrong place for the right thing. So we remain unsatisfied even as we become more possessive. We say out loud, to no one in particular, "Why am I not happier with all this stuff?"

This type of spontaneous outburst is a key moment in the spiritual life. On the lips of Adam and Eve it is a protest, but God takes it as a prayer. Out-loud ruminations, erupting from our suppressed spiritual nature and addressed to the wind, catch the ear of God. Questions that originate in our spiritual nature are the ones that God, who is Spirit, cannot resist. Although God cannot resist answering, we can resist asking. At least that is what Jesus thought. He put all the urgency and insistence on us getting on with it: "Ask, and it will be given you; search, and you will find; knock, and the door will be opened for you" (Lk. 11:9). It appears that Jesus knew what was in the human heart, for our turning to God usually only comes after we have turned unsuccessfully to everything else. The question "What are we? Asses tethered to a feeding trough? Oxen tied to a manger?" comes only after a lot of eating and drinking.

There is a real irony in the symbolic way Adam and Eve ask the question of their identity. They contrast themselves with the ox and the ass. This alludes to a divine tirade in the Book of Isaiah. The Lord is angry at Israel's disobedience and uses a homely barnyard image that has been incorporated into the lore of Christmas: "The ox knows its owner, / and the donkey its master's crib; / but Israel does not know, / my people do not understand" (Is. 1:3).[15] In the story, Adam and Eve are wondering if they are like beasts, a mindless digestive process. The very fact they are asking the question means they are beyond the strictly animal level. Their question is implicitly answered in the very asking. But in another way they know less than the animals. The ox and the donkey know where to feed their hunger. They know who their owner is and where the feeding trough is. However, Adam and Eve do not know this about themselves. They are a hunger and thirst that they do not know how to feed. They do not like being reduced to the ox and the ass, but, as Isaiah suggests, they could learn something from them.

This is the symbolic meaning of the ox and the ass in every crib set. They are the wise animals who show humans the place of nourishment. But they are not the only animals to show up at the birth of Christ. Isaiah also mentioned that kings with frankincense and gold arrive on dromedaries, so majestic camels stand by while their riders pay homage (Is. 60:6). Can there be shepherds without sheep? So sheep graze about and are probably the first to hear the shepherds proclamation of good news. Once an additive tradition starts, it is hard to stop it. In Christian imagination almost every animal has turned up at the manger—bugs, foxes, cows, dogs, cats and, with some very imaginative moves, miraculous air-breathing fish have made an appearance. In one French tale even the snake came to hiss homage. But, we are told, he was careful to stay away from Mary, whose heel he very much feared. The inventive genius of Christmas has turned the stable into a zoo.

Many of the animals are there just for the party. But some have keen insights into the meaning of the birth. My personal favorite is an animal who was never completely accepted in popular lore—the hog. Norma Faber has written a poem about his feelings:

Shall hog with holy child converse?
How will it feel?

Jesu dear
I lumber near.

You may yank my tail,
pull my ear.

I'll make you a small
silk purse.

The ox and the ass know who owns them and the place where they can find nourishment. The hog knows something equally significant. Conversation with the child can change a negative assessment of who you are into a positive appreciation of your hidden potential. If conversing with the child can "make a silk purse out of sow's ear," it can also turn a self-seeking man and woman into a self-giving couple.

The ox and the ass know that Adam and Eve are in search of a new feedbag. They are looking for their owner, the one who can give the nourishment they seek. This is a symbolic way of suggesting that the divine is integral to human identity. We are not constituted human and then related to God. It is our relationship to God that makes us human. This was Elie Wiesel's insight. "When he opened his eyes, Adam did not ask God: 'Who are you?' He asked: 'Who am I?'"[16] Augustine also coupled his desire to know God with his desire to know himself: "May I know You, may I know myself." This is also why Bede Griffiths can say, "The whole question is, what is the true Self?"[17] He knows that the true self necessarily implies the true God. Finally, this explains why the search for who we are leads to the child who is called the God-Man. If we only found the Son of Mary, we would not have the answer to our question. We must find the Son of Mary who is the Son of God. This seems to be the import of Galatians: "When the fullness of time had come, God sent his Son, born of a woman,…so that we might receive adoption as children" (Gal. 4:4). Finding the Son of Mary who is the Son of God is finding ourselves as adopted children of God.

Therefore, waking up to the question of who we are is ultimately waking up to the question of who God is. In this context, even though Adam and Eve ask about themselves, it is natural that God hears the question. However, the divine answer is more indirect and subtle than the human question. We may shout at the sky, but the sky does not shout back. It sends angels to start a series of events that eventually will invite us into a space where the answer will be given to us without rancor, without anxiety, and without thunder. The revelation will be gentle yet firm, the way a mother holds a newborn child, for it is only a gentle firmness that can calm us.

Hearing from the Shepherds

God does not send Gabriel to Adam and Eve. God sends power ("Gabriel" means "the power of God") to the one who prepares the feast, the linen tablecloth of Mary, who presents Jesus as sustenance for the journey. In order for Adam and Eve to go farther, they must come in contact with a spiritual tradition and community. This is not the much-dreaded "second-hand" experience of institutionalized religion. It is the heritage of women and men who have already walked the path that Adam and Eve are starting down. They know the rough and smooth of the road and their whole being is dedicated to every seeker.

This is the necessary correlation between personal experience and the collective tradition. Life itself can wake us up. The journey of enlightenment may begin with any number of experiences—the repetitious rhythms of flesh, the uncontrollable pull of sex, the consuming power of revenge, the vastness of earth and sky, the intrusion of pain, etc. Who knows what will trigger the process of decentering, of seeing through the illusion of separateness. Gandhi had just seen Indians forced to walk in the gutter so that white people could stroll down the sidewalk. He wrote, "It has always been a mystery to me how men can feel themselves honored by the humiliation of their fellow human beings."[18] In that moment he saw through the distortions of conventional understandings. I know of a man who returned home late one Saturday night. He had been cruising around in his car yelling insults at blacks. When he walked in the back door, his mother was there with a broom and began to beat him and cry out through her tears, "We're all God's children. We're all God's children." His out-of-control mother hitting him with a broom started him along a path that made him a prominent civil rights activist. If we are attentive, there are enough jolts in our growing up and growing old to startle us into a suspicion of our true underlying nature. Life itself begins the journey of awakening, but in order to continue the journey we need a spiritual tradition and community. Therefore it is fortuitous and, in a heavier interpretation, providential that the searching Adam and Eve should come upon shepherds. The shepherds have just found what Adam and Eve are looking for and do not know it: a child.

The shepherds are the leaders of the spiritual community and tradition. They are vigilant in watching over the flock by night (Lk. 2:8). They are often contrasted with the hireling who does not truly care for the sheep (Jn. 10:11), and one of their jobs is to keep the wolf from the door (Acts 20:28–29). But their most important Christmas role is to "make known what had been told them concerning the child" (Lk. 2:17) in such a way that "all who heard them wondered at what the shepherds told them" (Lk. 2:18). The shepherds encounter Adam and Eve and perform their proclamatory task. They tell Adam and Eve what the angel told them. They are merely passing along the message and adding their own enthusiasm. The message has two parts—an announcement of salvation and an invitation to see for yourself.

The announcement of salvation contains an astonishing claim. A child is born who is "a savior, who is Christ the Lord." This brief proclamation strings together three titles—savior, Christ, and Lord. These are impressive credentials, but they are also exceedingly vague. Throughout all four Gospels, Christological titles both attract attention and cause confusion. They are frequently used by Jesus' enemies who have distorted ideas about what they mean. Their true meanings become clear only when they are closely linked to the actual life, death and resurrection of Jesus. In the infancy narratives it is the sign that specifies the vagueness of the titles: "Let this be a sign for you: you will find a child wrapped in swaddling clothes and lying in a manger" (Lk. 2:12). This sign is not just accurate directions to find the right child. It is symbolic code for the correct understanding of the titles.

An announcement

of astonishing claims

must be accompanied

by an invitation

to personally enter

the mystery.

However, the code cannot be read by casual observers. It demands participation and, through participation, revelation. When it is penetrated and its truth is seen, the response is not the cerebral pleasure of solving a puzzle: "And the shepherds returned, glorifying and praising God for all they had heard and seen as it had been told them" (Lk. 2:20). Gratitude, that most personal and most overflowing of all experiences, is what happens. That is why any announcement of astonishing claims must be accompanied by an invitation to personally enter the mystery. Titles without experience will eventually be misunderstood. Therefore, it is not enough for the shepherds to penetrate the revelation, rejoice, and tell Adam and Eve what *they* had experienced. They must invite Adam and Eve to Bethlehem, to the house of bread, where *their* hunger can be fed and their thirst slaked. If they journey and find the child, they in turn can announce his titles and invite others to his manger.

In fact, this responsibility of giving away what you find was smuggled into the shepherds' announcement and invitation. They told Adam and Eve what the angel told them. A child is born "to you" and the good news is that he is meant for "all the people." The birth is an event with universal ramifications, but it is being announced to particular people at a particular time and in a particular place. How will the good news get to all the people except through the ones to whom the child has been born? To hear about the birth of Christ is to become a missionary for the birth of Christ. Perhaps Adam and Eve did not "bump into" the shepherds. The shepherds, filled with their own finding, sought them out.

I believe this is how most of us hear from God. We can get to God without any help from a spiritual tradition and community, but to hear from God we need to be in contact with those women and men who are especially gifted. We need shepherds who listen and take seriously the directions of angels. They are the frontrunners who have left markers along the way. They complement, articulate, validate and correct our intuitions. At their best, their spiritual traditions are not heavy-handed or authoritarian. They do not want us to praise their specialness; they want us to share their ordinariness. Their task is to seek out and welcome the earth-roamers, the ones who love the earth but realize that if they are to continue to love it they must deal with the perception that they somehow transcend it. If these earth-roamers are attracted to the Christian claims, they must immediately be given an invitation: "You will find a child wrapped in swaddling clothes and lying in a manger." And then comes the hanging moment, the second of decision, the instant of freedom: "Let us go over to Bethlehem and see this thing that has happened which the Lord has made known to us. And they went with haste" (Lk. 2:15).

You Will Find a Child...

Adam and Eve risk the journey. The story does not detail their motivation, but it seems to be a combination of the shepherds' enthusiasm and their own frustration. They have not found the answer to their question, but neither have they given up the search. Some consider this the ideal preparatory stage for spiritual insight. The way they presently see the world is inadequate, and they know it. This opens them to an alternate vision, makes them yearn for something more complete. They may not have a clear idea of *what* they want, but *that* they want is the steady driving force of their lives. Those who are more satisfied would probably pass up the shepherds' invitation. The earth-roamers are on their way to Bethlehem, looking for they know not what.

They find what the shepherds predicted—a child wrapped in swaddling clothes and laid in a manger. This is the central revelatory symbol in the infancy narratives of Luke. It is referred to three times, each time in a slightly different rendition. First, it is stated that Mary gave birth to her firstborn, wrapped him in swaddling clothes, and laid him in manger because there was no room for them in the inn (Lk. 2:6–7). Secondly, the angel announces that the shepherds will find a child wrapped in swaddling clothes and lying in a manger (Lk. 2:12). Thirdly, the shepherds arrive at Bethlehem and find "Mary and Joseph and the child lying in a manger" (Lk. 2:16). These images spark many ideas and feelings. We will explore them as the response to the search of Adam and Eve.

The child wrapped in swaddling clothes alludes to at least two passages in the Hebrew Scriptures. The one most often cited is from the

Book of Wisdom. King Solomon is reflecting on his common bonding with the whole human race. "In *swaddling clothes* and with constant care I was nurtured. For no king has any different origin or birth, but one is the entry into life for all; and in the same way they leave it" (Wis. 7:4–6). The focus of the entire passage is on common mortal humanity. If we take this as the key to the image, the revelation concerns the mortality of the Son of the Most High, his complete embrace of creaturely existence.

However, a narrower focus brings out a different meaning. Swaddling clothes are connected with constant care and nurture. This calls to mind a reference to faithless Jerusalem in Ezekiel. At Jerusalem's birth "your navel cord was not cut; you were neither washed with water nor anointed, nor were you rubbed with salt, nor *swathed in swaddling clothes*" (Ez. 16:4). The absence of swaddling is an absence of affection and love. The presence of swaddling clothes signals the child is beloved. This interpretation of Jesus as the beloved child is reinforced continually throughout Luke's Gospel. In particular, at the baptism and transfiguration the voice from the sky declares the true identity of Jesus: "This is my beloved son." What Adam and Eve find is a beloved child.[19]

The image of the beloved child taps into the overall child spirituality of Christian faith. The most common interpretation of child imagery is in terms of trust. However, trust in God has a much different feel from trusting in people or things. When we trust in people and things, we often prize them as permanent partners in a fickle and fading world. This is also true of God. The divine is an unfailing presence. However, the divine is always actual, always now. To trust in the actuality of God has the feeling of "letting go," of mid-air instability. Stephen Levine sees this natural trust with children in the playground:

This stage [being in transition] reminds me of children swinging across the monkey bars in a playground. Moving across the overhead trellis from one bar to the other with ease, one can see how easily children let go of the last and trust the next. Children seem almost to glide from one end of the bars to the other. But often, I'll notice a chaperoning parent come to play with their child on the monkey bars, attempting that same crossing. They don't move with such ease. They hang stiffly from one bar to the next. They will not let go of the last bar until they've grasped the next, dangling like a herniated chimp before falling to the ground. They don't trust the momentum that allows the next moment to appear as it will, without clinging to the last.[20]

If this is what Adam and Eve perceive in the beloved child, it should ease their anxiety. Their frustration and searching should not be evaluated negatively. They are in a natural process, a temporal process in which change and search are integral to human identity. They should try to move easily from stage to stage, trusting the swinging process rather than choking each bar in fear of falling. They must trust the process of questioning that arises from within and not see it as an unwanted intrusion into the comfortable world they have already established.[21]

In the Gospels this focus on trust is further clarified when it is contrasted with the drive to greatness. The disciples have a chronic question on their mind, "Who is the greatest?" Sometimes they phrase it piously, "Who is the greatest in the Kingdom of Heaven?" (Mt. 18:1), and sometimes it is just a matter of naked ambition, "They had been discussing among themselves who was the greatest" (Mk. 9:34). The way they think about greatness is in terms of exclusion and scarcity. If they can exclude the nongreat, for example little children (Mk. 10:13–16), or suffering and ignominy (Mk. 9:30–37), they will have achieved their goals. Or if they can have what others do not, for example, "Grant us to sit one at your right and one at your left when you enter your glory" (Mk. 10:37), then they will be great. The disciples are driven by the need to be important and significant. They want to be somebody. Every time this ambition surfaces, Jesus places a child in their midst or talks about a child.

This spontaneous human mechanism—the drive to be somebody—may lie beneath Adam and Eve's question and the fury with which they ask it. "What are we? Asses tethered to a feeding trough? Oxen tied to a manger?" is shot through with the fear of insignificance. The question is phrased in a comparative way—the relationship of Adam and Eve to the animals—because greatness is always thought of in relationship to others who are less great and so merit our disdain or to those who are greater and so merit our envy. To want to be somebody is to be caught between disdain and envy. How is the child wrapped in swaddling clothes an answer to the quest for significance?

The beloved child is the natural condition, a given of human existence. The child is loved as original and not as one in comparison with others.[22] Also the child is beloved before achievement, and therefore achievement is not the effort to gain greatness but the abundant overflow of the sense of being loved. To be beloved is not the conferral of status. Beloved "status" would just be another bar to hold on to. To be beloved is to be in union, loving union with the Source of Life. The child wrapped in swaddling clothes is not a message from God but the revelation of Adam and Eve's actual condition, the answer to their heartfelt shout, "What are we?" They are a living union with the divine.

To be beloved is

to be in union,

loving union with

the Source of Life.

Naturally, this child wrapped in swaddling clothes is laid in a manger. The manger is a feeding trough. It symbolizes the Gospel eucharistic themes of Jesus as food for the world. Jesus' identity, the identity of the beloved child, is to give himself to others for their growth and sustenance. This does not diminish him but enhances his powers. Sacrifice for others, making them holy, is not heroic self-denial but natural self-fulfillment. This is the way of God, and it becomes the way of the one united to God. If Jesus, the beloved child, wants to give himself that completely, there must be a way to receive him.

Mary knows the way. She is the perfect disciple, the one who knows how to be fed by the beloved child. Her own nurture is summed up in the activity of pondering the events of Jesus' birth in her heart (Lk. 2:19). The art of pondering, integrating and realizing is what she teaches Adam and Eve. They must touch the heart of the child. Once that is touched, they will be able to see what he sees (drink from his eyes) and realize the truth of his words (eat from his mouth). The bread who comes down from heaven is meant for earth-roamers.

However, the spiritual dynamism of feeding is no different from the physical dynamism of feeding. We are constituted by what we eat and drink. Once we are nurtured by Christ, we become what he is. He is not the only beloved child laid in a manger. That is the identity of all of us, an identity indebted to Jesus, the firstborn. Beatrice Bruteau spells out this totally relational identity:

> Each person is a transcendent "I am" which is identically a spondic "May you be," radiating life and love, the energetic will for abundant being, to each of the others. Each is an agape lover and loves the lover in each other person. For in willing good and abundant life to another person, what can we will more than that this person should be a vital lover also? Thus each lover lives by spiritually indwelling each other lover; each person exercises personhood by uniting with each other person's personhood. Fundamental to personhood is that it is interpersonhood.[23]

The last line of this densely symbolic story — "We tie ourselves to this manger'"—cuts two ways. Adam and Eve tie themselves to the manger in the sense that they will continually be sustained by Christ and ever more deeply realize his revelation. He is their food and drink. However, the ones who receive Christ also give Christ away. They tie themselves to the manger in the sense that they will be food and drink for others. They will seek to activate the beloved child in others. They began their journey by waking up to the mutuality of themselves with all creation, a mutuality based on their need for food and drink. They end their journey by realizing they have more than a craving for food and drink; they have a natural desire to be food and drink for others. That is a considerable and salvific transformation of consciousness. A few stanzas from the "Discourse on Good Will" capture this new awareness:

Just as a mother with her own life
Protects her child, her only child, from harm,
So within yourself let grow
A boundless love for all creatures.

Let your love flow outward through the universe,
to its height, its depth, its broad extent,
A limitless love, without hatred or enmity.

Then as you stand or walk,
sit or lie down,
As long as you are awake,
Strive for this with a one-pointed mind;
Your life will bring heaven to earth.[24]

The journey that began by waking up hungry and thirsty ends with the hungry and the thirsty becoming food and drink. Adam and Eve are now fully and luminously awake. You can hear their laughter and the playful irony in their voices as they chide the sky, "What are we? Asses tethered to a feeding trough? Oxen tied to a manger?"

Christmas Morning

The goal of the Christian spiritual life is articulated in the Gospels quite briefly and simply: "Love the Lord, your God, with all your mind, heart, might, and soul; and your neighbor as yourself" (Lk. 10:27). These words are often called the double commandment of love. When the emphasis is put on commandment, we hear the words as imperatives addressed to the will. However, they are best understood as adjustments to our vision. They express the true condition of creation, which we only glimpse in our estranged state. We are in union with God and neighbor but the scales need to fall from our eyes. The one who knows how to make this happen is Jesus. According to the great conciliar tradition, his reality is to be one in being with God and one in being with us. Therefore, the one who lives at the end of the journey—the realization of union—is a good guide for those who are still on the path. The one who is wide awake knows how to shake others from sleep.

If the goal can be simply stated and the guide can be confidently pointed out, the progress of our walking and the process of our waking is complex and tentative. The story of Adam and Eve is only one way. They began by noticing their hunger and thirst and sensing themselves as mutually interdependent. However, this horizontal solidarity did not satisfy them. Although they were immersed in creation, they sensed that they were more, but they could not account for this anguish of spirit in themselves. They began to roam, and their search led them to the shepherds and through the shepherds to the beloved child in the manger. This child fed them in a new way, a way that revealed to them their deepest identity. They were in union with God, and although the earth was their home it could never be their cage. They were meant to pour love into creation, not merely to participate in it out of need. Once they saw this clearly, they saw themselves. They woke up.

Our paths may be quite different from this road hacked out by Adam and Eve. But little by little we awake. More and more the hidden truth of every human gesture and word comes home to us. We hold a hand we have held many times, and suddenly it is a staggering experience. Or we notice we do not lose ourselves when we give ourselves away. We may lose time and money, but we ourselves seem to grow larger without any sense of arrogance. Or we cannot maintain our indifference to the pain of other people, no matter how much we tell ourselves that there is nothing we can do. Or we find ourselves talking to the air in words we did not plan, knowing there is someone listening but not knowing who. Or for some nameless reason we stretch ourselves out on the earth and just lay there, growing out of the ground. Whenever or wherever our consciousness breaks through to communion, it is Christmas morning. We are children and we have just awakened from sleep. It has snowed during the night and the earth is white and new and fresh. Dare we walk on it? There is a present under the tree. It is a gift for a beloved child. Dare we open it?

Chapter 4

Giving Birth to Christ

In the beginning the Great Spirit gave a box to all the animals. The box was painted with many sacred signs and symbols. Inside the box was a gift.

As the animals opened their boxes, all of creation tumbled out. Plants tumbled out, trees tumbled out, rivers tumbled out, streams tumbled out — everything appeared, and after some considerable confusion everything took its rightful place. It did not happen in a day. It took some time. But soon all the animals had opened their gifts.

All, that is, except the seagull.

The seagull tucked his gift box under his right wing, smiled smugly, and said, "The Great Spirit gave me this gift. It's mine. I'm not going to open it." There was no more explanation.

However, it did not take the other animals long to learn what was in the box of the seagull. For although all of creation had tumbled out, they could see none of it. For in the box of the seagull was the gift of light.

The fox approached the seagull and pleaded, "I have a burr caught in my tail, and I cannot see well enough to get it out. Please open your box." But the seagull only repeated his position. "The Great Spirit gave me this gift. It's mine. I'm not going to open it."

The bear came to the seagull and complained, "My hibernation schedule is off. I do not know when to sleep and when to wake. Please open your gift." But the seagull just gripped his box more tightly and shook his head.

The deer approached and asked, "May I speak personally? I have just been embarrassed. I was bounding through the forest with my children and I crashed into a tree and chipped an antler. I heard my children laugh.

135

It should not be this way. We need light. You must...."

"I must nothing," said the seagull. "It is my gift, is it not? The Great Spirit gave it to me, did he not? I won't open it."

The animals did not know what to do. So they went to the cousin of the seagull, the raven. The raven is a notoriously tricky bird, and they thought perhaps he might have an idea. He listened to their complaints, told them to go home, and said he would "look" into it. Then he laughed at his own joke.

The raven flew around until he sensed the presence of the seagull. He landed next to him, settling silently on his right side. "My cousin, the seagull," said the raven, "it is good to see you," and he laughed gently.

When the seagull heard it was the raven and knowing the raven was a tricky bird, he shifted the gift-box from his right wing to his left. He wanted to keep it as far away from the raven as possible. As he did, he lifted his right foot ever so slightly from the ground. The raven bent down quickly and slipped a thorn under the seagull's right foot. When the seagull shifted his weight back, the thorn pierced his foot. The seagull let out a great cry.

"What is it, my cousin?" said the raven.

"I have stepped on a thorn," said the seagull.

"That must be very painful," said the raven. "I know how tender are the soles of the feet of the seagull. Why do you not pull it out?"

"I would," sighed the seagull, "but if I try, I will drop the box which the Great Spirit gave me."

"Oh, I see the problem," the raven sympathized. "I would love to help you. But I cannot see well enough to pull the thorn from your foot. If I could see, I would certainly help you."

The seagull thought about this but could think of no way out. Carefully, he took the box which the Great Spirit had given him and opened the lid, just a crack. Instantly, a string of lights escaped and shot up into the blackness of the sky and strung themselves across it like a necklace. Creation was lit in starlight.

When the raven saw the earth shimmer under the stars, he let out an exclamation of wonder, "OOOOOOOOOH!"

"The thorn," interrupted the seagull. "You said you would take out the thorn."

"So I did," said the raven. The raven bent down, but instead of pulling the thorn out, he pushed it in. The seagull cried out a second time.

"I'm sorry," apologized the raven. "I'm sorry. But I could not see well enough. I could see enough to touch the thorn, but I could not see well enough to know whether I was pushing or pulling it. If I could see better, I am sure I could pull it out."

The seagull thought about this but could think of no way out. Carefully, he took the gift that the Great Spirit had given him and opened it a little wider. There emerged a small, brilliant ball, which slowly climbed into the sky. As it climbed, it grew bigger and bigger. Finally, it took its place among the stars. Creation was lit by moonlight.

When the raven saw the earth caressed by the light of the moon, he let out an exclamation of wonder, "OOOOOOOOOOOH!"

"The thorn," interrupted the seagull, "you said you would take out the thorn."

"So I did," said the raven. The raven bent down, but instead of pulling the thorn out, he pushed it in even further.

The seagull cried out a third time, and his wings flapped up in the air. The box that the Great Spirit gave him fell from his grip and banged against the ground. The lid flew open, and there fled from the box a golden, luminous ball, which streaked into the sky. The stars and the moon retreated before it. Finally, high in the sky, it stopped and blazed gently. Creation was lit in sunlight.

When the raven saw the earth bathed in sun, he let out an exclamation of wonder, "OOOOOOOOOOOOOH!"

"The thorn," the seagull said in a dejected voice. "You said you would take out the thorn if you could see. Surely, now you can see."

"I surely can," said the raven. He bent down and pulled the thorn from the seagull's foot.

The seagull sighed in relief, "OOOOOOOOOOOOOOOH!"

"There," said the raven, looking at the sparkling earth, "isn't that better?"

That is why, down to this day, to remind us how difficult it is to let the light that is within shine forth and illumine all creation, the seagull stands on one foot.[1]

This story, which has its origins in the Native American folklore of the Northwest, reads like a commentary on Jesus' words in Matthew's Sermon on the Mount: "You are the light of the world.... No one after lighting a lamp puts it under the bushel basket but on the lampstand, and it gives light to all in the house." The light of each person is not meant for themselves, but meant for all, that all might see better the other gifts of creation.

However, there is another theme in the story of the raven and the seagull. The seagull's light is held tightly. It is locked within the box that the Great Spirit has given him. The task of the raven is to help the light that is within move outside. The movement from the inside to the outside is a favorite theme of spirituality. The presupposition is that the person can unite with an interior transcendent love and then manifest that love in the exterior world. You can let the light shine before others, and if people perceive it correctly, they will see your good works and give glory to your Father in heaven. The reason they will praise God is that the ultimate source of the action will be divine love. In the symbolic code of Christmas, the acting person will give birth to Christ.

There are many ways to approach the spiritual dynamics of giving birth to Christ. The story of the raven and the seagull suggests that it is a process of letting go of what we already have. However, there is a deep resistance to releasing what we perceive as "ours." There is a need for a teacher, someone to show us the way and to help us loosen our grip. The raven is not everyone's ideal teacher. When this story is told in a group, there are always a number of people who are turned off by the raven's pain-inducing pedagogy. They often argue that the raven should have "talked" the seagull into opening his gift. They admit that his approach may be one way to release inner light from someone who is extremely reluctant. But what about one who is eager but still needs reassurance?

During the Christmas season, this eager one is the Virgin Mary and her teacher is the angel Gabriel. Their interactions are much different from the raven and the seagull. But the eventual outcome is similar—the light of the world is born. The sacred story of their conversation is often called "The Annunciation of the Birth of Christ." This, however, puts all the emphasis on the angel Gabriel, who is the announcer. Although a great many people have sighted angels and speak highly of both their silent presence and active help, very few identify with them.[2] Our empathy goes out to our fellow human, Mary, the announcee. As Jean Houston sympathetically puts it, "What could be more embarrassing than finding yourself pregnant with the Holy Spirit? It is a very eccentric, inconvenient thing to have happen."[3] Since Mary is a key character and our co-creature, she should have marquee status.

A more appropriate title might simply be "The Story of Gabriel and Mary." This title stresses the interaction between the characters, and although there are only two exchanges (three, if you count the author's generosity in allowing us to overhear Mary's thoughts), they are highly significant. The interactions deal with Mary's resistances and her final compliance. Gabriel does not get away with an unimpeded proclamation. He has to explain and, like most angelic attempts at explanation, his leaves much to be desired. It seems the angelic style of conversation uses a few human ploys. When Gabriel cannot get clearer, he gets louder. He may be a kinder teacher than the raven, but by our standards he could be a little more forthcoming.

From our point of view, the most appropriate title might be "The Angel and the Virgin." Although the story is about Gabriel and Mary, by extension it is about all of us. Angelius Silesius has the right question:

> *What does it profit me if Gabriel hails the Virgin,*
> *Unless he brings to me the very selfsame tidings?*[4]

What the angel and the virgin are talking about is how to give birth to the Son of the Most High. This is primarily Mary's honor and destiny, but in an analogous way it is an activity all Christians are called to engage in. An ideal predisposition for every reading or hearing of this tale might be: "to me the very selfsame tidings." John of the Cross suggests the same intimate connections between the Virgin and the contemporary believer, only with different imagery. He plays on the "no room in the inn" image and counsels a more welcoming approach:

> *With the divinest Word, the Virgin*
> *Made Pregnant, down the road*
> *Comes walking, if you'll grant her*
> *A room in your abode.*[5]

This teasing invitation means more than letting the "Pregnant Virgin" use our house. It means, at minimum, we are the midwives of the birth of Christ. Finally, Beatrice Bruteau states clearly that the story of the Angel and the Virgin needs to be interpreted as a story of Christian identity and human possibility: ·

> To recover the spiritual power of the myth [virginal conception], we
> have to understand that what it is ultimately doing is revealing the
> deep truth about ourselves. The stories are about us. It is to us that the
> angelic herald announces that through the power of the Holy Spirit we
> will bring forth from our emptiness divine life. Or, taking it another
> way, nothing has to come into us from outside; the secret of divine life
> is already within us and needs only to be accepted and nurtured.[6]

Put too flippantly, the story of the Angel and the Virgin can be read as a Lamaze class for believers. It is a training exercise for learning how to give birth to Christ.

Before we explore the conversation between the angel and the virgin, we need to spell out what we will be looking for, the presuppositions we bring to the text. Our concern is the dilemma of the seagull: how do we allow the light that is within to shine forth, to extend itself into the world of creation? In our contemporary secular world we are more comfortable stating this concern from the opposite end: Where does action come from? Is it possible to act out of a spiritual source and, if it is, how do we contact and coincide with this source? This question has Gospel roots. It is associated with "doing the will of the Father." In particular, it is a perspective that is present in the Lucan portrait of Mary. She is a woman of faith, and her faith is portrayed as an active and powerful way of releasing spirit into the world. She knows how to fulfill a secret desire of the human heart. She knows how to get pregnant by the Holy Spirit. An angel has taught her. Before we overhear their conversation and the angel teaches us as he is teaching her, we need to explore more thoroughly where action comes from and how Mary is a woman of faith.

141

Where Does Action Come From?

There is a story about a busy man who one day hurriedly headed out the door for work. In his path was his three-year-old son playing with blocks. The man patted the boy on the head, stepped over him, opened the door, and went outside. Halfway down the walk, a guilt bomb exploded inside him.

"What am I doing?" he thought to himself. "I am ignoring my son. I never play with him. He'll be old before I know it." In the background of his thoughts he heard the pounding rhythms of "Cat's in the Cradle," Harry Chapin's ballad to lost fatherhood.

He returned to the house and sat down with his son and began to build blocks. After two minutes, the boy said, "Daddy why are you mad at me?"

It is not only what we do, but where we do it from. Our actions come from different places inside us. These different places affect the quality and effectiveness of what we do. We may think the inside is of little consequence as we push into the outer world, but it can change the impact of our actions. "Steeling ourselves" and doing something is not the same as "opening ourselves" and doing the same thing. Playing blocks out of guilt is not the same as playing blocks out of love, and the difference is quickly spotted.

We do not often reflect on the interior source of our actions. We live in a culture that glories in analysis and strategy. We analyze situations in terms of their pluses and minuses, their resistances and possibilities. Then we design our interventions, marshal our skills, and act. Next comes evaluation, renewed analysis, and more strategy. These moves are hallmarks of rationality, and no way of acting is complete unless it takes them into account. However, this "outer-centered" mentality often obscures the "person-centered" dimension of all action. When we are continually objectifying our situation, we overlook our "soul-state." Yet it is always somebody who acts, and "where that person is at" greatly influences the quality of the action.

There is a story about a woman who took her aging mother into her home.[7] The mother had a stroke and needed time to recover. The daughter was very solicitous and painstakingly attentive to her mother's every need. Nevertheless, a terrible fight broke out—over a hard-boiled egg. In the middle of the war of words, the mother stopped short and asked, "Why are you doing all this for me anyway?"

It was the question of "from what place" is all this care coming from. The daughter began to list reasons:

> I was afraid for her; I want her to get well; I felt maybe I'd ignored her when I was younger; I needed to show her I was strong; I needed to get her ready for going home alone; old age; and on and on. I was amazed myself. I could have gone on giving reasons all night. Even she was impressed.
>
> "Junk," she said when I was done.
>
> "Junk?" I yelled. Like, boy, she'd made a real mistake with that remark. I could really get her.
>
> "Yes, junk," she said again, but a little more quietly. And that little-more-quietly tone got to me. And she went on: "You don't have to have all those reasons. We love each other. That's enough."
>
> I felt like a child again. Having your parents show you something that's true, but you don't feel put down—you feel better, because it is true, and you know it. I said, "You're right. You're really right. I'm sorry." She said, "Don't be sorry. Junk is fine. It's what we don't need anymore. I love you."

Her actions were coming from every possible place inside her except from the one place that her mother needed to have them come from—the place of love. This "place of love" is the spiritual source of action.

143

Finding the spiritual source of action is not the same as having the proper motivation. Motivation belongs to the region of the mind. The mind rationalizes, weighs, considers and calculates. It is always aware of outcomes and ready, at a moment's notice, to defend itself. The woman in the story has so many reasons for what she is doing that she impresses even herself. Like all of us she is a person of many and mixed motivations. Her mother's question should not be construed as looking for one more motive. The mother suggests a place so far beyond motive that it makes all reasons look like junk. This is reminiscent of what Thomas More tells his daughter in Robert Bolt's play, *A Man for All Seasons*. His daughter thinks that there is no good reason for him to act the way he is acting. He calmly replies that in the last analysis it is not a matter of reason but a matter of love. The mother in this story knows the truth of that remark.

The divine is perfect in itself, does not need anything, and therefore did not create with an ulterior motive.

The spiritual place of action, deeper than the mind, is not only the soul. It is what Eckhart calls the ground of the soul and what we have called here the right eye of the soul. It is a capacity in people made possible by their contact with divine largesse. This peculiar quality of God—abundance, magnanimity—played a surprising role in a venerable theological debate. The question was why God created the world. One strange answer to this question is that God did not have a "why" in creating the world. The divine is perfect in itself, does not need anything, and therefore did not create with any ulterior motive. She created to create. It is just simply the largesse of love, its abundance and magnanimity.

When we act out of that place where the right eye is in union with God, our actions are energized in a similar way. Although on the level of the mind there may be more motives than we can count, on the level of soul the action is essentially unconflicted. It simply flows or, in the contrasting yet complementary images of Eckhart, "boils over" and "melts." This overflowing is because the person has coincided with the overflowing Source and is riding a wave into the exterior world. Beatrice Bruteau contrasts actions done before and after the soul has been united to the divine:

> This is the interpretation I would put on the word of Swami Brahmananda that spiritual life begins with samadhi. It is only after one has realized the divine union that one can begin to live the divine life. Coinciding with the divine life and consciousness means, in a Christian context, participating in the divine activity of creating, so that the prayerful life becomes, when it is full and ripe, the active life in the world. This is not the same as the active life serving as a prayerful life, which it does as one is advancing toward a state of insight and union. There the effort of activity serves as a means of purification to the one who prays, a preliminary to the state of union. Here the activity is a consequence of the divine union and comes about not because of the nature, condition or situation of the one who prays but because of the nature and will of God. It is God who is active and creative, and therefore one who is united with God must perforce be active and creative with God.[8]

In other words, the source of action we are trying to uncover, and this is pushing the imagery to the breaking point, connects the right and left eye of the soul.

There is story that brings out another aspect of spiritual action.[9] A tall, strong man with a baseball bat entered the reception area of an alcohol and drug rehabilitation center. He was shouting obscenities and began banging the bat on the desks of the secretaries and admitting personnel. They jumped back and tried to get as far away from him as possible. One ran into the back room and phoned the police. As the woman who told me this story put it, "Suddenly the older woman who was the director of the center appeared." She walked right up to the screaming man waving the bat. She ducked under his arms and wrapped her arms around his chest. In a heartfelt voice she repeated over and over again, "Oh, you poor man! Oh, you poor man!" They stood together in that strange embrace for a while, and then the man began to sob. The woman led him to a chair. He slumped into it and waited for the police. He never let go of the baseball bat.

Perhaps this story is overly dramatic, but it shows the creativity and courage of actions that flow from the spiritual center. Actions from this source almost always exhibit engagement instead of fear and avoidance. The outside world does not dictate the terms on which the person will act. The response to violence will most likely be meet by flight or counter-violence. In the story the woman responds with disarming compassion. This is one of the ways the early church remembered Jesus: "When he was insulted, he did not insult in return. When he suffered, he did not threaten..." (1 Pet. 2:23). His inner freedom was greater than the outer coercion to respond in kind. This is part of what is meant when the Johannine Jesus consoles his disciples' fear with, "In the world you have tribulation, but cheer up, I have overcome the world" (Jn. 16:33). Overcoming the world is not allowing it to dictate the terms of engagement.

Spiritual actions are also what are called "actions in the way of things." They coincide with some power in the situation that is luring it to the best possible outcome. There is a mysterious partnership involved. The action is not a gesture in the wind. It attracts whatever in the universe makes for harmony and releases that power into the situation. As St.

Paul suggested, "All things work together for good" (Rom. 8:28)—once they are shown the way. What is at work is the persuasive power of God. What is at stake is the advent of the Kingdom of God. "Not everyone who says to me, 'Lord, Lord,' shall enter the Kingdom of heaven, but only those who do the will of my Father who is in heaven" (Mt. 7:21). The "will of the Father who is in heaven" is not a predetermined forecast of events to which humans must submit but an active coinciding with the transcendent power of love, which is secretly shaping the emergence of each moment. How to join and contribute to this emergent work is what every angel teaches every virgin. In other words, the angel is instructing Mary how to be a woman of faith.

A Woman of Faith

Augustine's comments on the "annunciation scene" in Luke have echoed down the centuries. "Mary, full of grace, first conceived Jesus in her heart before she conceived him in her womb.... The Virgin Mary did not have intercourse and conceive, rather she believed and conceived.... Mary in believing conceived without a man."[10] Others have picked up on this insight and talked about Mary "conceiving through the ear." In this interpretation the emphasis is on the primacy of faith and the power of faith to manifest itself in the physical world.

Augustine's insight is rooted in the portrait of Mary in the Gospel of Luke. In that Gospel, Mary is preeminently a woman of faith. Faith, however, is a word of many meanings. In fact, it can mean so much that it becomes increasing vague and communicates nothing. An attempt to narrow down its meaning often stresses that it is a series of attitudes of mind and heart in relation to the Word of God. Mary embodies these attitudes — obedience, openness, trust, meditation and perseverance. Still, this attitudinal rendition of faith does not get to the heart of the matter.

147

There is one episode in Luke that suggests the depth dynamics of faith. A woman shouts from the crowd, "Blessed is the womb that bore you and the breasts that nursed you!" But Jesus says, "Rather blessed are those who hear the word of God and keep it!" (Lk. 11:27–28). The standard interpretation emphasizes the contrast between blood ties and spiritual ties. It fits into the ongoing Gospel tension about who is Jesus' real family. Is it those who are physically related to him or those who, like himself, hear the word of God and keep it? The answer is that spirit takes precedence over blood.

However, there is a provocative alternate reading. When we read the text in the light of Mary, who is both the physical mother of Jesus *and* one who hears the Word of God and keeps it, more complementarity than discrepancy emerges. The tension is relaxed and an interrelationship comes into view. The spiritual understanding of the self remains primary. What is most important is realizing ourselves as rooted and integrated in the Word of God. But this realization naturally unfolds into the physical world. It is like a seed hidden in the earth that naturally grows into a bush and pushes itself into the visible light, like a seed hidden in a woman's womb that naturally grows into a child and pushes itself into the visible light. What is conceived in the world of spirit is manifest in the world of flesh. The one who hears the Word of God and keeps it inevitably gives birth to Christ and nurtures him.

Faith is ultimately about the integration of the spiritual and physical. Said another way, it is about the invisible and visible dimensions of the human person. The self as spiritual is hidden from sight. It is inside, an interior relationship with the Source of All There Is. The self as physical is "in plain sight." It is outside, the exterior way we deal in the world. We are one, but we can, so to speak, turn in two different directions. We can realize ourselves in these two mutually interlocking ways. In Chapter 1 we talked about this double turning as the two eyes of the soul. The right eye gazes at God; the left eye attends to the world.

Therefore, in the Gospel of Luke Mary is a woman of faith not only because she is obedient, open, trusting, meditative and persevering but also because she knows the intricate interaction of spirit and flesh. This is precisely the flow we want to explore. How does it happen? How do we resist it? How do we go along with it? What are the blocks and what are the breakthroughs? Eckhart says it boldly: "If Mary had not first given spiritual birth to God, he would never have been born bodily from her."[11] Mary knows the secret, but will she tell? The answer is that Luke is only too willing to tell us—but not clearly. He does not want to tell us *about* it. He wants us to participate in the reality. His symbolic story demands that we push and ponder until the angel is speaking to us and we are so troubled that we are asking Mary's hard questions, which, to push along the imagery nine months, are the strains of labor. "When a woman is in labor, she has sorrow, because her hour has come. But when she delivers the child, she no longer remembers the anguish, for joy that a child is born into the world" (Jn. 16:33).

Mary is a woman of faith not only because she is obedient, open, trusting, meditative and persevering but also because she knows the intricate interaction of spirit and flesh.

The Waiting Virgin

In the sixth month
the angel Gabriel was sent from God
to a town of Galilee named Nazareth,
to a virgin, betrothed to a man whose name was Joseph,
  of the house of David,
and the virgin's name was Mary.

In Luke's story Gabriel has been seen before. "In the sixth month" refers to his last visit. At that time he appeared inside the temple, at the right hand of the altar, to Zechariah, a priest who was chosen to burn incense at the time of prayer. Temple, altar, incense, priest, prayer—this is an expected setting for angels. Now the setting is a town so small (Nazareth) the larger territory must be mentioned first (Galilee) so that people will know where it is located. The visit is to a virgin of transitional social standing, betrothed but not yet living with her husband. This is an unexpected setting for angels. On the surface it seems the angel has visited both ends of the social spectrum. He is present in the temple and in the town, to the priest and to the virgin.

However, the priest and the virgin have something in common. They are both figures of longing. Gabriel's opening line to Zechariah is, "Fear not! Your prayers have been heard." Zechariah and his wife Elizabeth, though aged, have been praying for a child. They have disposed themselves and now wait for divine graciousness. Other characters in Luke's infancy stories are in the same position. Simeon and Anna, people also found in the temple precincts, await the salvation of Israel. In the first moment, this waiting signifies an eager openness for something to arrive. But it also entails cultivating the power of recognition. Elizabeth, Simeon and Anna recognize the child of Mary as the fulfillment of their waiting. Their waiting, even though it is open-ended, makes them fulfillment-ready. In Zeffirelli's *Jesus of Nazareth* Simeon is sitting in the temple when he suddenly hears the child Jesus cry out during the circumcision rite. He is immediately on his feet moving toward the hope that will allow him to say, "Lord, now you can dismiss your servant." Does salvation come to people who yearn for it or do people who yearn for salvation find it?

Mary's longing is symbolized by her virginity. There is a legend about Mary that explores this meaning of her virginity. The birth of Mary was the direct result of the prayers of her parents, Joachim and Anna. Therefore, at a young age she was dedicated to God and went to live in the temple. Mary's home was the temple and, eventually, God's home was Mary. The new temple grew up in the old temple and absorbed an overwhelming truth about the dwelling place of God. It is a truth that the Roman general Pompey could not absorb.

When Pompey conquered Jerusalem, he rode his horse into the temple and stormed into its most sacred precincts, the holy of holies. He was startled to find that it was empty. There were no images or artifacts, just empty space. This may have confused Pompey, but it instructed Mary. The ultimate dwelling place of God must be empty. Like the temple of stone, the temple of flesh has an inner sanctum, a holy of holies. It, too, is empty. Mary is a virgin.

Twice in the opening line of the story Mary is introduced as a virgin, and later she herself will make reference to her virginal status. At least at the beginning of the story virginity is the significant feature of Mary's identity. On the physical level, virginity means lack of sexual intercourse. For a woman this entails a certain physical intactness. On the social level, in ancient cultures the virginity of a woman meant nonattachment. She did not belong to anyone. In the story Mary is attached to Joseph, but Joseph's significant feature is that he is of the house of David. The house of David, which is a symbol of unconditional divine allegiance, will become central to Mary's developing identity, and so her betrothal to Joseph is not an instance of alien attachment. Rather it points in the direction of her longing. She is pledged but not yet married to divine love. She has not given herself away to any alien other. She is, like her son, a Jew of the first commandment: "I am the Lord, your God. You shall have no other gods before me."

The spiritual meaning of virginity takes its clues from the social meaning. Meister Eckhart writes: "It was necessary that it be a virgin by whom Jesus was received. 'Virgin' designates a human being who is devoid of all foreign images and who is as void as he was when he was not yet."[12] To be devoid of all foreign images is to return to essentially creaturely status, "void as he was when he was not yet." This means spiritual virginity entails a radical recognition of dependence on God. If we give ourselves over to foreign images and lose this type of virginity, we can regain it. Caryll Houselander tells us how: "We need to be reminded that every second of our survival does really mean that we are new from God's fingers, so that it requires no more than the miracle we never notice *to restore to us our virgin-heart* at any moment we like to choose."[13] Virginity as a physical fact either "is" or it "isn't;" virginity as a spiritual condition is a possibility of each moment.

Spiritual virginity is an emptiness that is simultaneously an openness, a psychic detachment that is also a psychic readiness. This is symbolized in the story by the fact that the virtue of Mary's virginity is not chastity but obedience. Mary hears the Word of God, listens wholeheartedly, waits expectantly. This generous receptivity is the result of virginal detachment. In common parlance, she keeps herself for the one she loves. Her emptiness is "like the hollow in a reed, the narrow riftless emptiness that can have only one destiny: to receive the piper's breath and to utter the song that is in his heart…an emptiness like the hollow in the cup, shaped to receive water and wine."[14] In the world of the spirit, virginity and fecundity are not opposite ideas but interrelated realities.

John Layard explores this close connection between virginity and pregnancy:

What then do we mean by "virgin?" It may help us to examine those ways in which we use the word that are not directly concerned with sex. We speak of a "virgin forest" as being one in which the powers of nature are untrammeled and untouched by man…. Thus in this sense the word "virgin" does not mean chastity but the reverse, the pregnancy of nature, free and uncontrolled.[15]

In this perspective, virginity suggests a natural pregnancy from divine fecundity. The virgin is one whom God makes fruitful without human aid. This is symbolically expressed by saying that the virgin is also a mother.

But at this point in the story, conception and motherhood have yet to occur. They await Mary's freedom. The emphasis is on virginity, not as a lack but as an active hunger—a waiting for One we cannot make arrive but whom we trust will appear. Then why do we wait? Anthony de Mello tells of an exchange between a master and a disciple:

"Is there anything I can do to make myself Enlightened?"
"As little as you can do to make the sun rise in the morning?"
"Then of what use are the spiritual exercises you prescribe?"
"To make sure you are not asleep when the sun begins to rise."[16]

Simone Weil, the prophet of mystical waiting, believed in the same paradox. "We cannot take a step toward the heavens…. If however we look heavenward for a long time, God comes and takes us up. He raises us easily."[17] Perhaps God sends angels to virgins because virgins are expecting them. Or perhaps it is that God sends angels to everyone but only virgins see and hear them.

The reason they see and hear them is that waiting is neither negative nor neutral activity. It is a formative practice that shapes human identity. Paul Tillich suggests how this works:

> Although waiting is not having, it is also having. The fact that we wait for something shows that in some way we already possess it. Waiting anticipates that which is not yet real. If we wait in hope and patience, the power of that for which we wait is already effective within us. He who waits in an ultimate sense is not far from that for which he waits. He who waits in absolute seriousness is already grasped by that for which he waits. He who waits in patience has already received the power of that for which he waits. He who waits passionately is already an active power himself, the greatest power of transformation in personal and historical life.[18]

Most renditions of the meeting of Gabriel and Mary have Gabriel intruding on the reveries of a shy young girl. Giotto's painting has Mary reading a book when Gabriel arrives. He interrupts her leisure. If we take the spiritual symbolism of virginity seriously, however, this is hardly the case. Mary is a handmaid of the Lord long before Gabriel's visit. She has turned away from many attachments and turned toward the vast, terrifying heavens. Historical approaches to the birth of Christ guess that Mary was a young woman of about fifteen. But the literary-spiritual symbol of virginity suggests that she was not an undirected adolescent. Gabriel met an eager-eyed woman: open, powerful, attentive, waiting—his match.

This opening scene of the story of the angel and the virgin connects longing and renunciation as the preparations for the spiritual life. There is in every person a desire to be intimate with the ultimate source of life. In some people this desire is strongly cultivated. They commit themselves to the house of everlasting love. This attachment naturally leads to detachment. They refuse to give themselves away to anything else. This does not mean they are not engaged in many activities and do not have many roles in family and society. It means none of these ultimately define them. They are free of them and so can relate through them. The longing for God and detachment from alien images is not the spiritual life. It is the "getting ready." As in the story, it sets the scene for something else to happen.

Favor, Mission, and Fear

> And entering he said to her,
> "Rejoice, O favored one! The Lord is with you!"
> She was greatly troubled at the saying
> and considered in her mind
> what sort of greeting this might be.

This encounter between Mary and the angel happens inside. The angel is pictured as *entering*. In fact, there is an emphasis on inwardness throughout the story. Mary is to conceive *inside* her womb without the aid of anything from the outside. She enters *into* the house of Elizabeth and greets her. When the sound of the greeting came *into* Elizabeth's ears, the baby *inside* her leapt with joy. This interior stirring unleashes the Holy Spirit. Elizabeth is thrilled with what the *inside* of Mary will produce ("Blessed is the fruit of your womb"). Mary responds by singing that the *inside* of her, her soul and spirit, is expanding and rejoicing. The "inside" imagery suggests that the angel addresses an inner, spiritual center.

The existential name of this spiritual center is "Rejoice, O favored One. The Lord is with you." This greeting carries two messages. Mary is both loved (the favored one) and sent (the presence of the Lord always entails mission). Gabriel reveals a divine love that is also an

155

It is the spiritual nature of the human person to experience favor and mission simultaneously.

active solicitation. His words are meant to empower. They are a call to action. Favor is for mission; divine presence is for divine purposes.[19] This is remarkably similar to the way the Matthean Jesus begins the Sermon on the Mount. He addresses people as "blessed," "salt" and "light," and then urges them to act in accordance with this identity. In other words, he is complimenting them at the same time as he is commissioning them. This is not just a ploy used by Gabriel and Jesus. It is the spiritual nature of the human person to experience favor and mission simultaneously. The preparation is over. This is the beginning of the spiritual life.

However, this greeting is not met with an enthusiastic "Here I am, Lord." Mary's response is a more realistic mix of fear and puzzlement. The text does not tell us explicitly where the fear and puzzlement come from. However, there are a few clues. And when they are combined with some general insights regarding the dynamics of the spiritual life, we can imaginatively develop a fuller picture of Mary's mind. It seems that Mary is troubled for a different reason than Zechariah. The mere sight of Gabriel caused Zechariah to be afraid. Quaking is a natural response to a supernatural presence. Before God, the creature shudders. Despite Madeleine L'Engle's wonderful suggestion, "In Scripture, whenever an angel appears to anyone, the angel's first words usually are, 'FEAR NOT!'—which gives us an idea of what angels must have looked like."[20] Mary is not unnerved by the mere sight of Gabriel. Mary is no stranger to sheer transcendence. Renunciation and longing have given her a strong taste of the "more" that lurks everywhere. She is troubled by the angel's greeting. It is what he has to say that disturbs her.

We must remember that the greeting of the angel about intimate favor and mission is heard by a virgin. Mary's virginity meant that her identity was a mix of longing and renunciation. This combination of not giving herself away and standing ready for arrival heightened her individuality and developed a strong sense of soul. It is an initial and partial grasp of soul, but it is a "heady" experience of transcendent identity:

> Where we do sense our souls…is in our discernment of our individuality—the fact that from conception to birth we are the same person, a person distinct from all others.… The soul is the final locus of our individuality. Situated as it were behind the senses, it sees through the eyes without being seen, hears through the ears without being heard. Similarly it lies deeper than mind. If we equate the mind with the stream of consciousness, the soul is the source of this stream; it is also its witness while never itself appearing within the stream as a datum to be observed. It underlies, in fact, not only the flux of mind but all the changes through which an individual passes; it thereby provides the sense in which these changes can be said to be his. No collection of the traits I possess—my age, my appearance, what have you—constitutes the essential "me," for the traits change while I remain in some sense myself. To switch to the vocabulary of George Herbert Mead, the fragments of self that present themselves for identification constitute the "me" while the "I" that supports them as a clotheshorse supports the garments we drape over it remains concealed.[21]

The process of uncovering soul entails a sequence of negations. "I" am not my eyes, ears, mind, age, appearances, etc. What is left, the witness of my attributes, is often invested with the status of "This is me!"[22] Identified with soul, I think I am hidden and concealed. What is known are the garments, but the real "me" is the supporting clotheshorse that cannot be seen. A byproduct of increasing our identity with soul, however, is a growing loneliness. The inner life is empty and so are we. This emptiness has not yet become fullness. It has not turned into what John Donne called a "blessed nullification." It is just nullification, and strange to say it is its own elixir. We can get high on the self-mastery and freedom of this first stage of the spiritual life. We can learn to love the placid lake in the center of our being and its quiet, untroubled waters. When this happens, we identify with our nonattached virginal status and forget that motherhood is in the making. Therefore, what happens next disturbs us.

Suddenly an angel appears, not in the night sky but inside this solitary citadel. The story merely says he enters, but it can have the feel of a break-in. The front of the soul is the sense of individuality that looks outward, but the back of the soul, unknown to us, opens onto a divine ground that relates everything there is to everything else there is. This opening is how angels get in. They enter, to use another metaphor, through that room in the back of the heart that Chesterton saw so clearly, the Christmas room that holds something that "betrays us into good." The cause of fear is not the entry but the loving intimacy that overturns the loneliness we have come to identify with. The waiting virgin is no longer alone.

Rainer Maria Rilke's poem's captures what it is that stirs fear in Mary:

> Not that an angel entered (mark this)
> was she startled. Little as others start
> when a ray of sun or the moon by night
> busies itself about their room,
> would she have been disturbed by the shape
> in which an angel went;
> she scarcely guessed that this sojourn

is irksome for angels. (Or if we knew
how pure she was. Did not a hind, that,
recumbent, once espied her in the wood,
so lose itself in looking, that in it,
quite without pairing, the unicorn begot itself,
the creature of light, the pure creature—.)
Not that he entered, but that he,
the angel, so bent close to her
a youth's face that his gaze and that
with which she looked up struck together,
as though outside it were suddenly all empty
and what millions saw, did, bore,
were crowded into them: just she and he;
seeing and what is seen, eye and eye's delight
nowhere else save at this spot—: lo,
this is startling. And they were startled both.
Then the angel sang his melody.[23]

Intimate love where none was suspected: "that he, the angel, so bent close to her / a youth's face that his gaze and that / with which she looked up struck together…eye and eye's delight, / nowhere else save at this spot." The transcendent self, forged through negation and longing, has company. This is a new identity, and the initial response is agitation and fear. It may be what we have waited for, but arrival is always more than waiting. It is this strange experience that ends Annie Dillard's wonderful Christmas essay, "God in the Doorway": "So once in Israel *love* came to us incarnate, stood in the doorway between two worlds, and we were all afraid."[24]

In order to understand Mary's fear more deeply, we must consider some of the inherent tendencies of the mind. "Mary was greatly troubled at the saying and considered in her mind what this greeting might mean"—Mary is distinct from her *mind*, but she is actively engaging her mind to sort out her feeling-response of trouble. The reason for this is that feelings are cognitive-dependent. They are grounded in assumptions and ways of thinking. If Mary can notice the moves of her mind, she can uncover the cause of her feeling of anxiety. In the spiritual life, the mind must become a servant of a deeper love, not the conditioned determiner of our feeling states. When fear rises in us, the mind has always played a part, whether we know it or not. The mind is skittish; it leaps at any sound it cannot immediately identify; it has a knee-jerk reaction that even the knee would envy. The more we know about the mind the more we know about how fear comes for dinner and stays for breakfast.

The mind is a grocer. This was the opinion of Zorba the Greek, who was not known for his shy and retiring style. It makes lists. It wants everything orderly and predictable. It always has a plan "B" and many times a plan "C." It also has what might be called identity fever. It always wants to know who it is and where it is going. Therefore, it tends to make boundaries, draw tight circles, and turn temporary stages into permanent states. When news arrives that disrupts the tidy world the mind has created, it runs around like Chicken Little screaming, "The sky is falling! The sky is falling!" When the functioning of the mind is observed in the spiritual life, one of its recurrent patterns is to prematurely construct an identity and then be fearful when experiences happen that do not fit within its self-definition. This is not a flaw, just one of the ways the mind stabilizes the flow of life. We inhabit many temporary dwellings that the mind is tempted to pretend are forever.

Perhaps this conditioned trick of the mind can account for Mary's sense of fear. It turned detachment and longing into a identity description rather than a stage in the development of spiritual power. In the spiritual life what is achieved at one stage must be sacrificed in order to enter the next stage. Actually what must be left behind is our attachment to the stage we have become comfortable with. It is the old story. Every peak we attain is only a momentary plateau from which we spy another peak. In another image, the mind clings. Although at certain moments clinging has its advantages, it must always be in tandem with letting go. If the mind with its clinging tendencies is too much with us, the prospects of letting go cause fear. Christian asceticism has stressed disciplining the body so that it can serve the purposes of spirit. The mind is in similar need of attention. It needs to be lovingly embraced from a higher place so that it does not turn into a tyrant.

Besides the sudden identity shift from loneliness to love and her clinging mind's immediate panic, Mary's fear may also have come from the angel's suggestion of an unspecified mission. These divinely designed missions have the reputation of sending people places they do not want to go. In scriptural stories of divine and angelic commissioning, the human partners usually object. They are too young or not worthy or cannot speak well or lack experience or do not have the resources that *seem to be* necessary to undertake the task. These objections are instantaneous and often very persuasive. But the impression is that no matter how well founded their weakness is, the real reason for their hesitancy is that they envision a future that they cannot control: "When fears are examined, they can usually be traced to a thought, an image, or a fantasy about what might or might not happen in the *future*."[25] What if Pharaoh says no? What if the people say, "Who sent you?" What if I am asked to speak in public? The mind not only clings to temporary stages as if they were permanent states. It also manufactures futures that terrorize us.

When the mind directs its gaze on the unknown future, it spins fearful scenarios that put us into a chronic state of worry. This worrying about the future prohibits our awareness of the living present. Spiritual traditions continually point out this problem. One of Jesus' most memorable teachings contains this contrast: "Do not worry about your life, what you *will* eat or what you *will* drink, or about your body, what you *will* wear.... *Look* at the birds of the air..." (Mt. 6:25–26). He ends this teaching with a piece of dark humor that has helped many people rein in the runaway mind: "Let the day's own trouble be sufficient for the day." Attending to the present, watching it emerge, and contributing to its creation, is one of the premier skills of the spiritual life. It is also one of the best ways to become aware that the terrors of the unknown future are born and nurtured by the mind.

There are many learnings about the spiritual life in this episode of the story. Strange to say, we find ourselves troubled by divine favor and mission. When we explore this trouble, we notice our conditioned mind is working overtime. It has constructed an identity out of where we were, and so it does not want us to go forward. It attaches our identity to outworn models and is disturbed when the flow of life insists we move on. It is also fearful of a future it cannot control and creates dragons at every turn in the road. This may or may not be what troubles the literary and laconic Mary, but it troubles many who pursue the spiritual life. How will the angel-guru get us beyond this impasse?

Everlasting Love

And the angel said to her,
"Do not be afraid, Mary,
for you have found favor with God.
And, behold, you will conceive in your womb and bear a son,
and you shall call his name Jesus.

He will be great and will be called the Son of the Most High,
and the Lord God will give him the throne of his father, David,
and he will reign over the house of Jacob forever,
and of his kingdom there will be no end."

Gabriel immediately addresses Mary's fear. He knows that for any communion to happen fear must give way. Fear closes us down, makes us shrink back. We pull into ourselves, tighten the circle of our mind, freeze our feelings. Gabriel's strategy is to assure Mary of her favored status. He reinforces her new identity and shows her the direction it will take. The divine is not only the initiator of this event. God will see this action through to an end that will be "no end." In theological language the act of creation is continued through the act of providence and eventuates in everlasting life. Mary might have been responding to the unspecified mission out of her previous identity of the individual and lonely soul. The angel replies that the days of being alone are over. Favor is forever.

In one way this bypasses Mary's mind. It does not explain how her virginity is valued yet transcended, or detail strategies for dealing with the future. In the spiritual life, the mind dealing with the mind is a limited approach. We can substitute one set of ideas for another set of ideas, and if the substitute set is more in line with our identity boundaries, we feel placated. That is, until the next set of disruptive thoughts emerge. Then a new battle breaks out. No matter which set of ideas wins, our identification with our mind is strengthened. We think we are what we are thinking. That is why changing the contents of the mind is not as effective as relating to the mind, whatever its contents, from a different space. The angel avoids the morass of mind games and employs a process that has been called "putting the mind in the heart." He pushes beyond the place of fear, the conditioned mind, and addresses the deeper Mary. "Do not fear, *Mary*, you have found favor with God." The love that dissolves fear knows our name, and the name is deeper than both the fear and the conditioned mind that generates and sustains it. Only the heart, our relatedness to divine love, can handle the mind and its round-the-clock manufacturing of anxiety. It is this "space," this space of *Mary*, that the angel continues to address with love.

To be in touch with the divine is to enter into an everlasting life-giving process.

As the new love identity is reinforced, the mission associated with it grows in clarity. St. Bernard called Gabriel's words to Mary a "happy kiss" because they revealed a love that generated Christ. When we unite with divine love, fear is cast out (1 Jn. 4:18) and we naturally conceive and bear the Son of the Most High. God's love is always fruitful. The nature of the divine is fecundity. To be in touch with the divine is to enter into an everlasting life-giving process, a rule that will not be overcome by forces of destruction, a kingdom that has no end. This is what is meant by the symbol of "the throne of his father, David."

The Davidic covenant is often contrasted with the Sinai covenant. The Sinai covenant began with Yahweh's love and liberation of Israel and Israel's gratitude for its freedom. This initial love was sealed in a treaty with legal obligations. This covenant presupposed the separation of the two partners and bound them to one another by a series of laws. The essence of this covenant was the interaction of promise and requirement, grace and demand. If Israel kept the commandments, plenitude followed. If Israel broke the commandments, devastation resulted. The two partners always remained separate, and their history is a combination of a lover's quarrel and a lawyer's debate. Both pointed to the tablets of stone between them, Yahweh demanding obedience and Israel claiming exemption, feigning forgetfulness, pretending compliance, and actually struggling to live up to its side of a very demanding agreement.

The Davidic covenant was different. On the surface the mutuality seemed to be lost. God pledged himself unconditionally to the house of David. God would never abandon David. This was more a statement about

God's fidelity than it was about David's righteousness. God is an eternal creative energy at work in and through the human. God does not threaten withdrawal or punishment. This does not mean the human partner is merely an observer or that God is indifferent to the lack of response. In order for the Son of the Most High to be born there must be cooperation. Mutuality is essential, but the dynamics of mutuality with an everlasting lover are different from the give and take of a treaty partner.

Just what does the human partner have to do? That is Mary's question.

Unblocking the Mind

> And Mary said to the angel,
> "How can this be, since I do not know man?"
> And the angel said to her,
> "The Holy Spirit will come upon you, and the power of the Most High will overshadow you.
> Therefore, the child to be born will be called holy, the Son of God.
> And, behold, your kinswoman Elizabeth, in her old age has also conceived a son; and this is the sixth month with her who was called barren.
> For with God nothing is impossible."

"How can this be, since I do not know man?" is one of the most famous questions of the Gospels. However, its meaning is not all that obvious. Eugene LaVerdiere has suggested that the angel's announcement is the proper context for Mary's question.[26] This means the important word is not "how" but "this." The "this" refers back to the entire statement of Gabriel, in particular the remark that Mary will give birth to a child who will be called the Son of the Most High. It is not just a question of

165

how she will have a baby without sexual intercourse. It is how she will be the mother of the Most High without sexual intercourse.

This emphasis also changes the meaning of Gabriel's response. The angel is not explaining to Mary how the pregnancy will occur, nor is he reassuring her that God will be with her. He is not addressing her words directly. He is replying to the framework within which they are spoken. His response brings to light an assumptive world that needs to be corrected. Hidden in Mary's question are at least two assumptions. Both assumptions block the possibility of conceiving the Son of God.

The first assumption is that Mary must initiate the conception. She thinks she must do something in order to give birth to the Son of the Most High. The angel tells her that, on the contrary, she must let something happen. What she must let happen is the descent of the Holy Spirit. When she opens herself to the power of the Most High, new possibilities of life will emerge. This is not a passive posture. It is a creative act of coinciding with the power of the divine. It is not the abdication of Mary's self-direction but the joining of her self-direction with the self-direction of God.

This overlapping of the divine and human is a way of communing, of becoming one. This coinciding is clearly seen in the Greek text. "Nothing is impossible with God" literally but awkwardly reads, "Every *word* of God's is not without power." Mary's response is effectively, "Let that *word* be my word." If we ask whether God or Mary is the most active, the remark of Reginald Fuller is appropriate, "Mary's response was one hundred percent affected by the grace of God, yet at the same time it was one hundred percent her own act of submission."[27] Or, in terms of the classic saying, "The wind of God is always blowing, but you must raise your sail." The task of human consciousness is alignment with divine intention. When this happens, "what is born of you shall be called holy."

The second assumption hidden in Mary's question has a long history. It is present in the story of the prediction of a son for the aged Abraham and Sarah. This story from the Book of Genesis is often seen as the prototype for the story of Elizabeth and Zechariah. Both couples are beyond childbearing age, both are told by representatives of the Lord that they will have a son, and both, in various ways, are disbelieving. Gabriel mentions the barren Elizabeth's pregnancy as a way of surfacing and unblocking Mary's way of thinking. The mindset of Mary's question may not be far from the mindset that produced Sarah's laugh.

Sarah's laugh is a delightful episode that combines "tell me another one" human skepticism with steady divine patience. One of the visitors to the tent of Abraham and Sarah predicts that the aged couple will have a son. When Sarah hears this, she laughs to herself, "Now that I am withered and my husband is so old, am I still to have sexual pleasure?" The Lord asks, "Why did Sarah laugh?... Is anything too marvelous for the Lord?" Out of fear Sarah replies, "I didn't laugh." But this denial was seen through. "Yes, you did," was the response.

Sarah laughs because she knows the way of things. Women her age do not conceive. Why? Because there are physical laws that rule the human condition. They are absolute and unalterable. It is laughable to think they can be transcended. This line of reasoning may be expressed in this ancient text, but it is also a contemporary sentiment. The physical world is a closed system of causes and effects. Within this system certain things are possible and certain things are impossible. Barren women bearing sons is not one of the possible things.

What is often not noticed in this "case for the impossible" is that our minds have constructed it. We assume that we are speaking objectively about the world as it is, but actually we are speaking about the world as we construe it. Possible and impossible are mental categories, not physical ones. The mind creates the boundary between the possible and the impossible, and that boundary is a moving line, as the history of scientific achievement shows. The first thing to note is that Sarah is dealing with her own mind. She is scoffing at the possibility of new life because of the limits she herself has imposed.

Imposing limits is what limited people do. It is to be expected. God, on the other hand, who is unlimited, does not exhibit the same tendency. In Dennis McFarland's *The Music Room*, Raymond is telling Marty about what his dead brother, Perry, told him about the difference between God and man:

> Marty, there was something Perry said that day we talked. It was so nutty and I was so taken with it I wrote it down. Perry told me to look around the room I was sitting in. It was the kitchen—I remember I was sitting at the counter, you know, where the bird has his cage? So I looked around and Perry said, "Are you looking around?" and I said yes. Then he said, "Just think, Raymond. Every single thing you see, before it existed in the world, it first existed in somebody's mind." And I started thinking, well, it was true, wasn't it? But then I saw your mother's parakeet and I said wait a minute, Perry, what about the bird? And he said the parakeet first existed in the mind of God, and the cage first existed in the mind of man, and that was the difference between God and man. He was always coming out with stuff like that—you know, nutty stuff—but it was never about God before.[28]

Perry recognizes the flow from mind to matter, but he also recognizes the difference between the human mind, which encages life, and the divine mind, which opens life up.

The core of Sarah's mental assumption is her severing of the physical world from its spiritual source. She thinks that everything can be accounted for when reality is viewed as a series of predictable physical responses. Biblical faith embodies the opposite assumption. The material world is not its own explanation. It came forth from God and is sustained by God. The divine has not withdrawn and the world is not operating on independent laws, not even laws put there by God. What we perceive are partial connections that continually are superseded by larger perspectives and more complex integration. The only law is that the intimate and unbreakable relationship between the spiritual and the physical makes all things possible.

This is a radical perception and one that is difficult to maintain. It means that God continues to speak the word of creation at every moment, and if God wishes to speak a new word then God may. As Martin Luther put it, "Just as God in the beginning of creation made the world out of nothing, so His manner of working continues unchanged."[29] Physical reality may appear to work on its own, but its origin, continuance and destiny are from the world of spirit.

Frederick Sontag tries to make this jarring perspective more credible by connecting it with the better known processes of human creativity:

At God's command, the world sprang into view. Why not? Voice is the outward form of spirit and words are the spirit's concrete manifestations. Spirit through words assumes new substantial form. Why not? It happens in human creative activity every day.... Spirit can give voice, we know that, and words or symbols properly activated can produce physical change and even create physical substances out of ideas. Composers do it. Set designers do it. Politicians do it. Why not conceive of God's activity in the world along similar line, the spiritual connection?[30]

If this is how the divine works, it is also how the divine and the human work together. We realize ourselves as spirit by uniting ourselves with the power of God. In the first moment this communing is an interior act of surrender. But it does not remain an inward love affair for long.

The purpose of the union is birth. The spiritual self unfolds into physical manifestation. In the life of the spirit first there is communion, then there is manifestation. Word precedes action: "In the beginning was the Word," but also "the Word became flesh" (Jn. 1:1, 14).

This is what Sarah eventually learns. The order of creation is spirit, word, and then physical reality. It has been said that Sarah laughed once, then denied it. Then she laughed a second time at the birth of Isaac, whose name means laughter. This time she had no reason to deny it. The first is the laughter of confinement; the second is the laughter of transcendence. It is this lesson of the second laugh that Gabriel brings to the mind of Mary.

It is also time for another response. Mary has been troubled, and the angel, in his own way, has tried to calm her. She has asked a question, and the angel, in his own way, has stated that it is a question based on faulty assumptions. In other words, he is clearing away obstacles, relativizing her fears, and unblocking her mind. It is time for Mary to talk.

Yes!

And Mary said,
"Behold, I am the servant of the Lord.
Let it be to me according to your word."
And the angel left her.

Some medieval meditations add to the encounter of Gabriel and Mary a host of heavenly onlookers. They are hanging over clouds and fluttering in mid-air. They are eager and expectant, awaiting the consent or refusal of Mary, a consent or refusal that will determine the course of salvation. In some renditions they are cheering Mary on, praying for her, encouraging her, calming her fears, telling her that all generations will call her blessed if.... In other words, this meditation, for all its imaginative fun, takes Mary's freedom very seriously. Gabriel may have come on strong, unrolling a parchment of proclamation about the birth of the Son of the Most High, but this does not mean it is a done deal. Giving birth to Christ is not a result of forced entry.

It is the freedom and courage of Mary that Denise Levertov highlights in her poem "Annunciation":

> We know the scene: the room, variously furnished,
> almost always a lectern, a book: always
> the tall lily.
>
>   Arrived on solemn grandeur of great wings,
> the angelic ambassador, standing or hovering,
> whom she acknowledges, a guest.
>
> But we are told of meek obedience. No one mentions
> courage.
>   The engendering Spirit
> did not enter her without consent.
>   God waited.
>
> She was free
> to accept or to refuse, choice
> integral to humanness.
>
> Aren't there annunciations
> of one sort or another
> in most lives?

Some unwillingly
undertake great destinies,
enact them in sullen pride.
uncomprehending.

More often
those moments
                when roads of light and storm
                open from darkness in a man or woman
are turned away from
in dread, in a wave of weakness, in despair
and with relief.
Ordinary lives continue.

                God does not smithe them.
But the gates close, the pathway vanishes.

She had been a child who played, ate, slept
like any other child—but unlike others,
wept only for pity, laughed
in joy not triumph,
compassion and intelligence
fused in her, indivisible.
Called to a destiny more momentous
than any in all of Time,
she did not quail,
                only asked
a simple, "How can this be?"
and gravely, courteously,
took to heart the angel's reply,

perceiving instantly
the astounding ministry she was offered:

to bear in her womb
Infinite weight and lightness: to carry
in hidden, finite inwardness,
nine months of Eternity; to contain
in slender vase of being
the sum of power—
in narrow flesh,
the sum of light.

                Then bring to birth,
push out into air, a Man-child
needing like any other,
milk and love—
but who was God.

This was the minute no one speaks of,
when she could still refuse.

A breath unbreathed,
            Spirit,
                    suspended,
waiting.

She did not cry, "I cannot, I am not worthy."
nor, "I have not the strength."
She did not submit with gritted teeth.
                raging, coerced.

Bravest of all humans,

consent illumined her.

The room filled with its light,

the lily glowed in it,

and the iridescent wings.

Consent,

courage unparalleled,

opened her utterly.[31]

In the last analysis the human openness to bring forth Christ is an act of courage. Of course, after courage has propelled us into the world of action, we find allies everywhere. Goethe is right: "Until one is committed there is hesitancy—the choice to draw back—always ineffectiveness.... [But] the moment one definitely commits oneself then Providence moves too. All sorts of things occur to help that would never otherwise have occurred. A whole stream of events issues from the decision, raising in one's favor all manner of unforeseen incidences and meetings and material assistance which no one could have dreamt would have happened." Then, of course, in the light of this unforeseen help, we declare that the issue all along was trust. It may be trust in hindsight. That is what Elizabeth tells the pregnant Mary: "Blessed is she who trusted that the Lord's word to her would be fulfilled." But the virgin on the edge of pregnancy centers on the love she knows and leaps toward the world she does not know. She exclaims, "Look at the one who rides God like a river." When Gabriel hears this, he leaves immediately. His mission is accomplished; hers is about to begin. The virgin is pregnant.

A lot has happened in this conversation between the angel and the virgin. A detached and longing person has discovered divine love at the center of her being. This revelation signals a new stage in her identity and demands she leave behind a towering sense of transcendence for an intimate sense of communion. This communion means mission, because the One to whom she is united is an ever-overflowing reality. This One promises an everlasting presence but is strangely silent about particulars. If there is to be a birth, what the virgin must do, in one sense, is get out of the way. This does not mean passivity but a decentering that steadily focuses on divine initiative. When we coincide with this energy, we become who we are meant to be and manifest God in the flesh. This is what Thomas Merton means when he says Mary is *in the highest sense a person* precisely because she does not "obscure God's light in her being."[32] That, in the last analysis, is what the story is trying to teach us—how to be a person in the highest sense.

Chapter 5

The Magi Ride Again

In the mid-1960s, a Roman Catholic cardinal and a priest Scripture scholar found themselves seated at the same table at a dinner party. The cardinal immediately put forth his grievance. "You know, Father, there are some Scripture scholars these days who are saying we don't know how many Magi there were."

"I am not one of them," replied the scholar.

"I'm glad to hear that…"

The cardinal did not have a chance to finish.

"There were six." The scholar opened the palm of his hand and shrugged his shoulders in a "what can I tell you" gesture.

"Six!" blustered the cardinal. "How do you figure six?"

"Well, in the reliquary at Cologne there are the heads of three wise men and in the reliquary at Milan there are the heads of three wise men. Three plus three equals six."

Although this anecdote is probably fictional, it gets big laughs where academics gather. I don't know if anyone has told it at a bishops' meeting.

The number of the Magi is not given in Matthew's account. In Christian imagination they have ranged from two to a whole cohort. But in most Nativity art, from earliest times to the present, there are three. It seems natural that three gifts should have three carriers. Can all those crib sets be wrong?

This question of numbers may seem to be a bit of trivia reserved for dining with clerics, but the conversation definitely heats up when someone suggests that the number was zero. It is contended that the story of the Magi is legendary, that it has theological importance but no basis in history. People who have held this opinion have received unexpected

Christmas gifts. Raymond Brown, a prominent Roman Catholic Scripture scholar, remembers that "one such magi-bunker received a hand-painted Christmas card depicting three very angry Orientals in royal garb, accompanied by camels, knocking at the door of his study, demanding by name to see him."[1] At Christmas we pray for Christ to be born in our heart. Is it an added bonus for the Magi to appear at the door?

If the Magi reduce historical reason to silence, they thrill the artistic imagination to song.

The question of the historicity of the Magi story in all its aspects—where exactly in the East did they come from; how could Herod have assembled the chief priests and the scribes; why did Herod ever let them go; what type of star was it; what happened to the gold, frankincense and myrrh?—will continue to be explored and debated. Our concern is not with the scarcity of historical data but with the abundance of poetry and story. If the Magi reduce historical reason to silence, they thrill the artistic imagination to song. Where the historian legitimately equivocates, the poet and storyteller legitimately expound.

The historian adjusts his glasses and notes the Magi have no names. The storyteller takes another tack.

"Names! Names! Of course, no names are given by Matthew," the storyteller throws up her hands in exasperation. "If Matthew gave the names, the vicious descendants of Herod would know who they were and be able to trace and slaughter their children and their children's children. No, their names were kept secret for centuries until it was safe. I can tell you now that they were called Gaspar, Melchior and Balthazar. It is time for all to be known. The truth, as Jesus said, is at home on the rooftops. So my story begins with the truth of the Magi's own births so that you will see how it was that they came to search and sacrifice for the birth of Christ...."

Or what does the word "Magi" suggest? Philologists vacillate among alternatives—deceivers, magicians, astrologers or philosophers. The storyteller only sees options. "I think I will make them magicians frustrated by their own magic, searching for the one person for whom words and gestures are not tricks. No, wait, they have come to find a king. Then kings they too must be. Kings acknowledging *the* King. Surely, that is the meaning of it all."

The Magi arrive from the East, but there is no mention of their mode of transportation. Where the cultural historian investigates the travel habits of the ancient world, the storyteller suddenly sees horses, Arabian horses of exquisite beauty. Or camels, desert ships sailing on moonlit sands. Of course, these bearers of Magi bearing gifts will talk to each other. They have complaints and dreams too, and they will not be left unaffected by the baby and his mother. After all, have they not borne the burden of the gifts? Do they, too, not have hearts fit for worship?

Which reminds me of the mouse who smuggled herself into the saddlebag of Gaspar's camel, Lucky. She was a teenage mouse who had had a terrible fight with her parents....

Part of this is just plain fun for the storyteller and, hopefully, entertainment for the storylistener. But depending upon the storyteller and the ambition of the story, part of it is a faith-inspired enterprise. The Magi become symbolic carriers of Christian perceptions, vehicles of Christian insights. This may not be the mainline way of expressing and communicating Christian faith. More sober and direct catechetics is always needed and, at least on some occasions, is definitely preferable. But what storytelling lacks in directness it makes up in invention and expansion. The Magi may be dubious as historical facts, but in the Christian tradition they have been credible bearers of rich insights into strange ways of faith.[2]

Of course, the original story in Matthew is the touchstone text. It is a tale steeped in irony, laden with symbols, and rich in theological associations.[3] However, the popular Christian tradition never felt unduly tied to Matthew's text. The story became more a springboard for the imagination than an anchor for sober reflection. In a generous estimate, it might be said that the original story initiated a trajectory of concerns that later elaborations developed. However, a more accurate appraisal might be that the Magi of popular poetry and story are more indebted to the concerns of Christian faith in general than to the dynamics of the brief tale in Matthew 2:1–12.

This fact does not devalue the Magi stories. It places them in their proper perspective. They do not claim to be an authentic interpretation of Matthew or a reexpression of divine revelation. Yet they do try to tell the truth about some of the common patterns of our lives. They try to make good on the Isaian promise that is connected with the feast of the Epiphany: "The people who walked in darkness have seen a great light; upon those who dwelt in the land of gloom, a light has shone" (Is. 9:1). In other words, the Magi stories and poems illumine shrouded areas, areas where the pains and promises of life are mixed together.

We will explore what the Magi have to say about some of these areas. In Christian tradition the Magi have embodied the danger of alienated reason, the always puzzling paradox that we grow old yet remain the same, the realistic appraisal that life is a hard search that often ends in an unlikely find, the perception that there is a depth communion that relativizes our differences, the intuition that material gift-giving is really about spiritual meeting, and the bittersweet experience that strangers often remind us of our true identity. In Matthew's story the Magi came primarily to worship; in subsequent tradition they rode again, driven by desires not far from any human heart.

The Alienated Mind

G. K. Chesterton wrote an essay on three modern Wise Men.[4] They journeyed to a city of peace, a new Bethlehem. They wanted to enter this city and proffered their gifts as passports of admission. The first put forth cold gold and suggested it could buy the pleasures of the earth. The second did not carry frankincense. He brought instead the modern scent of chemistry. This scent has the power to drug the mind, seed the soil, and control the population. The third brought myrrh in the shape of a split atom. It was the symbol of death for anyone who opposed the ways of peace.

When they arrived at the palace of peace, they met St. Joseph. He refused them entrance. They protested, "What more could we possibly need to assure peace? We have the means to provide affluence, control nature, and destroy enemies." St. Joseph whispered in the ear of each individually. They went away sad. He told them that they had forgotten the child.

This tale is a critique of contemporary wisdom. The Wise Men come with the benefits of wealth and technology, and they think that those assets will bring peace. The story is suspicious of these gifts, but it does not deprecate them. It views them neutrally, suggesting that in themselves they will not provide access to the city of peace. The real problem is not what the modern Wise Men have brought, but what they have not brought. They have forgotten the child.

The enigmatic symbol of the child points to the missing ingredient of modern wisdom. The child image pushes the mind and heart in many directions. It is difficult to know which path will prove productive. A poem of Chesterton's entitled "The Wise Men" provides some clues:

> Step softly, under snow or rain,
>   To find the place where men can pray:

The way is all so very plain
That we may lose the way.

Oh, we have learnt to peer and pore

On tortured puzzles from our youth,
We know all the labyrinthine lore,
We are the three wise men of yore,
And we know all things but the truth.[5]

It seems that Chesterton's concern is that the modern mind for all its sheer knowledge is divorced from something very simple. Later in the poem this "missing something" is a road "so very simple / That we stray from it" and "something too large for sight / And something much too plain to say." We are missing the obvious. He encourages humility:

Go humbly, humble are the skies,
And low and large and fierce the Star;
So very near the Manger lies
That we may travel far.

When we finally arrive at the missing truth, it will shake the heavens with laughter. "For God Himself is born again, / And we are little children walking / Through the snow and rain."

The problem is that our mind is not humbly at home on the earth. It is not rooted in the graciousness of divine presence. It does not understand itself as an expression of spirit. It knows everything except the most important thing—it is a child of God in both snow and rain. It can do everything except exult in its finitude. Peace will not be won by our affluence and technology until we know the earth as our home and all people as inhabitants of a common house.

Chesterton ends his poem "The House of Christmas" with precisely this insight:

> To an open house in the evening
> Home shall men come,
> To an older place than Eden
> And a taller town than Rome.
> To the end of the way of the wandering star,
> To the things that cannot be and that are,
> To the place where God was homeless
> And all men are home.[6]

The Wise Men need the baby to save them from their own knowledge. The mind that is alienated from the earth is never life-giving. The Magi need to enter into the house where Mary and the child are or else they will journey forever over the earth and never be at home. When they worship the God who lives on the earth, the mind that studies the sky will be saved.

To Each Their Own and To All the Same

There is a legend that the Magi were three different ages. Gaspar was a young man, Balthazar in his middle years, and Melchior a senior citizen. When they approached the cave at Bethlehem, they first went in one at a time. Melchior found an old man like himself with whom he was quickly at home. They spoke together of memory and gratitude. The middle-aged Balthazar encountered a teacher of his own years. They talked passionately of leadership and responsibility. When Gaspar entered, a young prophet meet him with words of reform and promise.

The three met outside the cave and marveled at how each had gone in to see a newborn child but had met someone of his own years. They gathered their gifts in their arms and entered together a second time. In a manger on a bed of straw was a child twelve days old.

The message of Christ talks to every stage of the life process. The old hear the call to integrity and wisdom, the middle-aged to generativity and responsibility, the young to identity and intimacy. The revelation accompanies us. We marvel at its richness and adaptability. To find Christ at any stage in our lives is to find ourselves.

Yet when all enter together—the young, middle-aged, and old—we find a deeper truth. No matter where we are in the life process, we are still children of God. We are newborn from the hands of God at every moment. Our dependency and indebtedness does not go away with maturity. There are many stages in the life of a human person, and each stage present different struggles and opportunities. Yet at each stage there is a permanent child. When we go in separately, we know we are in different places and different times. When we go in together, we know that even though we are different we are the same.

The Hard Search, the Unlikely Find

The Magi are searchers. They are looking for the Christ child, but they do not have exact directions and they cannot travel by day. A star leads them, a tiny point in a night sky. Their quest is mainly darkness and minimally light. They are manipulated by Herod and become unwitting accomplices in a horrible slaughter. They rejoice at their find and they present their gifts worshipfully, but they leave quickly and return home by another route. Darkness and danger are more a part of their lives than joy and worship.

Their situation is often contrasted with the shepherds. The shepherds do not have to deal with a mute star. They are blessed with a very talkative angel. This angel gives them exact directions to the birthplace of the child.

They will not have to consult devious kings. They are also told the identity of the child and serenaded with a song about the meaning of his birth. Once they arrive everything is exactly as they were told. They skip off to tell everyone, and to a person everyone is astonished at what they hear. Angelic revelation, joy, and proclamation tells the shepherds' story.

We may yearn to enter into the Christmas mystery with the simplicity and directness of a shepherd, but often the struggling Magi are our real representatives. Their struggle is characterized in many ways. Evelyn Waugh sees in their journey the vacillations of the learned:

> How laboriously you came, taking sights and calculating, where shepherds had run barefoot!... Yet you came and were not turned away.... For his sake who did not reject your curious gifts, pray always for the learned, the oblique, the delicate. Let them not be forgotten at the Throne of God when the simple come into their Kingdom.[7]

"Taking sights and calculating" is a tame estimation of the Magi journey. William Butler Yeats sees it as an endless, unsatisfied passion to ground our "thrashings about" in mystery:

> Now as at all times I can see in the mind's eye,
> In their stiff, painted clothes, the pale unsatisfied ones
> Appear and disappear in the blue depth of the sky
> With all their ancient faces like rain-beaten stones,
> And all their helms of silver hovering side by side,
> And all their eyes still fixed, hoping to find once more,
> Being by Calvary's turbulence unsatisfied,
> The uncontrollable mystery on the bestial floor.[8]

However it is rendered, the Magi are symbols of the restless human spirit, of the unseeing quests we undertake, and more often than not of the unlikely finds we discover.

T. S. Eliot's poem "The Journey of the Magi" is a classic tale of endless restlessness and the cost of finding what you search for:

A cold coming we had of it,
Just the worst time of the year
For a journey, and such a long journey:
The ways deep and the weather sharp,
The very dead of winter.
And the camels galled, sore-footed, refractory,
Lying down in the melting snow.
There were times we regretted
The summer palaces on slopes, the terraces,
And the silken girls bringing sherbet.
Then the camel men cursing and grumbling
And running away, and wanting their liquor and women,
And the night-fires going out, and the lack of shelter
And the cities hostile and the towns unfriendly
And the villages dirty and charging high prices:
A hard time we had of it.
At the end we preferred to travel all night,
Sleeping in snatches,
With the voices singing in our ears, saying
That this was all folly.

Then at dawn we came down to a temperate valley,
Wet, below the snow line, smelling of vegetation,
With a running stream and a water-mill beating the darkness,
And three trees on the low sky.

And an old white horse galloped away in the meadow.
Then we came to a tavern with vine-leaves over the lintel,
Six hands at an open door dicing for pieces of silver,
And feet kicking the empty wine-skins.
But there was no information, and so we continued
And arrived at evening, not a moment too soon
Finding the place; it was (you may say) satisfactory.

All this was a long time ago, I remember,
And I would do it again, but set down
This set down
This: were we led all that way for
Birth or Death? There was a Birth, certainly,
We had evidence and no doubt I had seen birth and death,
But had thought they were different; this Birth was
Hard and bitter agony for us, like Death, our death.
We returned to our places, these Kingdoms,
But no longer at ease here, in the old dispensation,
With an alien people clutching their gods.
I should be glad of another death.[9]

This poem articulates the Christian sensitivity that birth and death interlock. The hardness of the search is matched by the hardness of the birth that proves to be a form of death. We may romanticize this process of change, symbolized by birth and death, until we have undergone it. Then the most appropriate words are: "I should be glad of another death."

Following Christ costs. This is a Gospel theme that is stressed and restressed. Jesus' parables of the buried treasure and the pearl suggest that finding and selling go together, "going he sold all that he had...." To follow Jesus one must leave occupation and family. This is not so much a literal leaving as a symbolic detachment. Choosing a new absolute point of reference entails letting go of previous absolutes. To walk a new path we must leave the old path. This emphasis on detachment is not only insisted on in the Gospel, it seems to be the commonsense consequence of freedom.

Yet the inevitability of this painful process always stuns us. We are always taken by surprise that this newborn child wants whatever gifts we have. On the positive side, this means redirecting our energies toward whatever is coming to birth in him. On the negative side, it means letting go of other gods. The birth of Christ brings the awareness that we are alien people clutching gods.

"Clutching alien gods" is a classic way of saying we have misplaced our ultimate allegiance. The way we live is not grounded in the truth. But it is the way we know, the way we are comfortable with, the way our family and friends do it. Quite simply, it is the way we are. But now we have seen the birth and can no longer be comfortable in this old dispensation. The deeper problem is we cannot be comfortable in the new dispensation either. The voices keep singing in our ears, "this was all folly." The dilemma of these Magi is that they know the old will not work, yet they lack the courage to risk the new.

Another Wise Man who has a hard time of it is Artaban in Henry Van Dyke's *The Story of the Other Wise Man*.[10] This is a stylized tale, employing visions and revelations, and written in overblown prose. It moves toward a climatic ending that can be seen coming from quite a distance. Yet it carries a genuine Christian sensitivity and drives it relentlessly home.

Artaban is a Median, a follower of Zoroaster, and a worshiper of Ahura-Mazda. He has seen the sign in the sky and tries to convince his friends to join himself and Gaspar, Melchior and Balthazar in the search for the newborn king of the Jews. He is unsuccessful, but the old Abgarus encourages him with realistic wisdom: "My son, it may be that the light of truth is in this sign that has appeared in the skies, and then it will surely lead to the Prince and the mighty brightness. Or it may be that it is only a shadow of the light and then he who follows it will have only a long pilgrimage and an empty search. But it is better to follow even the shadow of the best that to remain content with the worst." This is the true sentiment of the searcher. It is better to search and come up empty than to settle for something less.

Artaban sets off to join his three fellow Magi and follow the star of their destiny. But he does not arrive at the meeting place in time. On the way he comes across a sick and dying Hebrew. He thinks to himself, "Should he risk the great reward of his divine faith for the sake of a single deed of human love? Should he turn aside, if only for a moment, from the following of the star, to give a cup of cold water to a poor, perishing Hebrew?" He attends to the man with all the skill of a physician. The man recovers, blesses Artaban, and tells him the prophecy of the Bethlehem birth.

When Artaban finally arrives at Bethlehem, Joseph, Mary, and the child have fled to Egypt and his fellow Magi have returned home. He is given lodging by a young mother with a newborn baby. While he is there, Herod's soldiers descend on the village and begin their slaughter. In order to save one child, Artaban bribes a soldier with a jewel he had hoped to give to the Christ child.

Artaban decides to continue his search for the newborn king of the Jews. This search takes him throughout the ancient world. Wherever he goes, he attends to the sick and needy. He spends his wealth on all those in need. This search goes on for thirty-three years. It finally leads him to Jerusalem. He has one jewel left, a pearl of great price.

When Artaban arrives in Jerusalem, he hears that they are going to crucify a man who is called "the king of the Jews." He realizes this might be the child of his quest and moves to join the crowd as they push toward

In the search

for Christ

we are already

experiencing him,

but in an

incognito form.

Golgotha. But once again his journey is cut short. A group of Macedonian soldiers are dragging a young girl down the street. She is to be sold into slavery to pay off her debts. She begs Artaban to help her. He gives up his last jewel, the pearl of great price, to ransom her.

Suddenly there is an earthquake. A tile shaken from a roof strikes him and he falls to the ground. As he lay dying, the girl he had ransomed holds him in her arms. She hears a faint voice. Then the old man's lips move and he says, "Not so, my Lord. For when saw I thee hungry and fed thee? Or thirsty and gave thee drink? When saw I thee a stranger, and took thee in? Or naked, and clothed thee? When saw I thee sick or imprison, and come unto thee? Three and thirty years have I looked for thee; but I have never seen thy face, nor ministered to thee, my King." The journey of Artaban is over.

The most blatant theme of this story is that the presence of Christ in basic human needs goes unrecognized as we search for the historical figure of Jesus. But there is a subtheme that is instructive for the searcher. The search may be its own reward; the struggle may be the goal. In the search for Christ we are already experiencing him, but in an incognito form. The task may not be to gauge the distance we have still to travel to find what we are looking for, but to be attentive to what is happening to us as we travel. Spiritual journeys are often struggles to awaken to what is already there. "When did I see you…" is the statement of darkened consciousness. "As long as you did it…" is the expression of enlightenment.

The World of Communion

When people attempt to summarize the revelation of Christianity, they often talk in terms of reconciliation. The divisions within people, between people, between people and the earth, and between people and God have been overcome. There is a new sense of communion. What was divided is now seen to be in a new, life-giving relationship. Communion has replaced separation. This awareness of communion includes claiming aspects of ourselves and others we had previously pushed away. The "peace" of the Christian greeting symbolizes the inclusion of what had been excluded.

This theme of communion and the overcoming of separation appears in some of the poetry about the Magi. In W. H. Auden's Christmas Oratorio, *For the Time Being*, the Wise Men and the shepherds both appear at the manger. Their voices are initially contrasted. The Wise Men talk of hunting high and low, traveling with doubt and the unknown, and finally finding an ending to their endless journey at the manger. The shepherds are the opposite. They talk of traveling nowhere, living in uninterrupted routine, and finding a beginning of their journey at the manger. They represent different types of people, but also they refer to different dimensions of each person.

For both these human types the birth of Christ is a refusal and a blessing. The Wise Men desire to have no past and the shepherds no future. These desires are refused, but it is noted that "Love" has used these escapist tendencies as a "guard and a guide." Instead they are both asked to bless their overriding drives, the Magi their impatience and the shepherds their laziness. Then they bless each other's sin and exchange places. The Wise Men give away their exceptional conceit and the shepherd's their average fear. Their final words are said together:

Released by Love from isolating wrong,
Let us for love unite our various song,

Each with his gift according to his kind
Bringing the child his body and mind.[11]

It seems that the journey ends in a sense of complementarity, a fullness of human life that combines Magi motion and shepherd rest. Love releases us from the isolating wrong of our own fate by connecting us to the song of others. This allows us to offer all we are, our body and mind, to the purposes of God. Only the gifts together make possible the gifts individually. The Magi's journey ends at the manger, but what they really find are the shepherds, the lost partners of their one-sided passion.

This same theme of communion is expressed in Christopher Pilling's provocative poem "The Meeting Place (after Rubens: *The Adoration of the Magi 1634*)":

It was the arrival of the kings
that caught us unawares;
we'd looked in on the woman in the barn,
curiosity you could call it,
something to do on a cold winter's night;
we'd wished her well—
that was the best we could do, she was in pain,
and the next thing we knew
she was lying on the straw
—the little there was of it—
and there was this baby in her arms.

It was, as I say, the kings
that caught us unawares....
Women have babies every other day,
not that we are there—

let's call it a common occurrence though,
giving birth. But kings
appearing in a stable with a
"Is this the place?" and kneeling,
each with his gift held out towards the child!

They didn't even notice us.
Their robes trailed on the floor,
rich, lined robes that money couldn't buy.
What must this child be
to bring kings from distant lands
with costly incense and gold?
What could a tiny baby make of that?

And what were we to make of
was it angels falling through the air,
entwined and falling as if from the rafters
to where the gaze of the kings met the child's
—assuming the child could see?

What would the mother do with the gift?
What would become of the child?
And we'll never admit there are angels

or that somewhere between
one man's eyes and another's
is a holy place, a space where a king could be
at one with a naked child,
at one with an astonished soldier.[12]

The revelation is that the space between people's eyes is holy, a place of unity between what is seemingly incapable of being reconciled. Those who know the full Christian story cannot read the last line of this provocative poem without thinking of another astonished soldier, a centurion at the foot of the cross. In the Gospel of Mark, that shocked soldier exclaimed that Jesus was truly the Son of God. Jesus is the Son of God precisely because he is able to pull together all the disparate threads, to bring into unity what is scattered, to hold in relationship a dying man and his executioner. Both the birth and the death of the Son of God reveal a world of communion.

The black poet Langston Hughes plays upon the theme of racial unity in "Carol of the Brown King":

Of the three Wise Men
Who came to the King,
One was a brown man,
So they sing.

Of the three Wise Men
Who followed the star
One was a brown king
From afar.

They brought fine gifts
Of spices and gold
In jeweled boxes
Of beauty untold.

Unto His humble
Manger they came

And bowed their heads
In Jesus' name.

Three Wise Men
One dark like me—
Part of His
Nativity.[13]

The background for this poem of inclusion is a profound theology of incarnation. In Christ God has united himself to human nature. The implication of this union with God is that all people are united with one another. In the last analysis they participate in the same reality. The differences between people are not as great as this common ground of life in Christ. To be "Part of His / Nativity" is to know yourself as reborn to a life of inclusive relationships. The Brown King, more than anyone else, knows this truth about the birth of Christ.

The Perfect Gift

Many years ago G. K. Chesterton took issue with Mary Baker Eddy, the founder of the Christian Scientism. Mrs. Eddy told the press that at Christmas she did not give presents in any gross, material sense. Rather she meditated on Truth and Purity till all her friends were better for it. Chesterton accused her of being anti-Christian. The whole point of the incarnation was to embody goodwill. "The Three Kings came to Bethlehem bringing gold and frankincense and myrrh. If they had only brought Truth and Purity and Love there would have been no Christian art and no Christian civilisation."[14] Chesterton goes on to argue that Christ himself was a Christmas present, a real embodiment of divine love.

Therefore, gift giving is the way the invisible becomes visible, the way the hidden heart is made known, the way spirit risks itself in substantiation. The gift giving that is associated with the birth of Christ is not gross, but spiritual activity of the highest order.

In Christian tradition the gifts of the Wise Men have become symbols of the perfect gifts. What makes them perfect is their ability to bear and communicate spirit. On the one hand, the gifts show that the Magi know who the child is. The gold symbolizes his kingly humanity, the frankincense his divinity, and the myrrh (an ointment used in embalming) foreshadows his redemptive death. They are not fooled by the outer trappings. Their gifts show they discern his inner reality.

On the other hand, poets have interpreted the gifts as symbols of the Magi's inner dispositions. Gold means that they offer their virtues, frankincense shows them to be people of prayer, and myrrh represents their willingness to sacrifice. The outer gifts tell of their inner reality. What is hidden is revealed. Their gifts are perfect because they allow communication between two interiors; the hearts of the Magi reach the heart of the child. The perfect gift is one that carries one person into another person.

This understanding of the perfect gift relativizes the gift itself. It may be a music box or a set of glasses or a sweater or book ends or a reindeer or even Santa Claus socks. What is important is not what it is but what it is capable of carrying. Does the gift make a meeting of spirits happen? This insight is simply expressed in Edmund Vance Cooke's poem "The Perfect Gift":

> It is not the weight of jewel or plate
> Or the fondle of silk or fur,
> But the spirit in which the gift is rich
> As the gifts of the Wise Men were.
> And we are not told whose gift was gold
> Or whose was the gift of myrrh.[15]

The gift itself is secondary to the world of spirit it is capable of communicating.

Storytellers have tried to communicate this insight by stressing the objective worthlessness of a gift that becomes subjectively priceless. The Little Drummer Boy is poor. He has nothing of value to give to the Christ child. So he plays his drum and the objectively worthless "boom, boom, boom," becomes subjectively priceless. In "Charlie Brown's Christmas Story," Charlie goes in search of a magnificent tree for his Christmas party. What he eventually finds is a broken down tree with one sagging ornament. Yet it is this tree that brings the kids together and opens up for them the spirit of Christmas. When the gift is objectively valuable, it may be desired for itself. In religious language, it becomes an idol, blocking rather than facilitating the flow of spirit. When the gift has no value in the eyes of the world, it may become priceless to the eyes of faith, eyes sensitive to the spiritual meeting of people.

No story brings this truth home more poignantly than O. Henry's *Gift of the Magi*. It is a story about a couple named Jim and Della. Although they are poor, they each have a proud possession. Della has beautiful long hair and Jim has "The Watch." As Christmas nears, Della cuts her hair, sells it, and buys Jim a "platinum fob chain" for his watch. When she gives it to him, Jim reveals that he has sold his watch and bought her a set of "pure tortoise shell" combs for her hair.

This story ends twice, both times with the same message. When Jim realizes what has happened, he plopped "down on the couch and put his hand under the back of his head and smiled." He tells Della the irony and ends with, "And now suppose you put the chops on." The smile and the comic return to the need for food reveal they both know what O. Henry makes explicit in the second ending. "Of all who give and receive gifts, such as they are the wisest." They are wise because they have both received something absolutely useless on the level of flesh and absolutely priceless on the level of spirit. Paradoxically, they have each received the perfect gift, both of them know and are known, love and are loved. They have received the gift of the Magi.

The Truth of the Stranger

Magi only journey at night
like the guarded secrets of dreams
and, at morning, always arrive from the East,
the rising sun at their backs,
haloing them in light.
You will have to shade your eyes
to watch them,
step by step,
approach you
with their request.

They are not wise in usual ways.
They cannot make a chair,
their soups are regrettable.
It is conjunctions
    symmetries
    balances
that interest them.
Heaven shakes, earth quakes.
As above, so below.
A star moves across the sky
and they are in the saddle
convinced an earth child
has yanked a string.
They come from a country of kites.

They also puzzle prophecies,
living in perpetual pregnancy,
awaiting the births of the predicted.
They unroll ancient parchments
to find new babies,
then read the wrinkles of the newborn
as testimonies of the past promises.
They are not your average observers.

That is why they have come to you—
        why they come to us all.
Your replacement has been born.
They need your help
to tell them
where
they can find the child.
Lost in higher logic,
they will not see you blanch
or notice you are troubled.
They want to teach you the lost art of homage,
how freeing it is to be prostrate before promise.
They are the strangers
who have come to tell you
the truth
you have forgotten.

Do not try to trick them,
coaxing from their enthusiasm
murderous information.
It will not work.

Wise Men always go home
by another route.
You will end
by slaughtering hope
and you will not see
the fleeing child, your child,
reach for their gifts.[16]

Matthew's story of the Magi is built on a massive, many-layered irony. The Magi Gentiles, through their own calculations, know about the birth of the king of the Jews. The Jewish leaders who have the prophecy of the birth in their Scriptures are ignorant of it. In the last analysis, these two groups need one another. The Jews need the Gentiles to alert them to the truth in their midst. The Gentiles need the Jews to show them the path to the truth they have discerned in the stars. The birth of Jesus is the fulfillment of the promises of both creation and covenant. He is the child of earth, meant for all people. But he comes from the people of the Jews, a child of the covenant. He is a universal savior born of a particular people.

However, this major message of the story is the background for darker and more complex confrontations. The strangers come to Herod with an outrageous request. They want him, the *present* king of the Jews, to help them find and pay homage to the *newborn* king of the Jews. They want Herod to provide them with directions to his replacement. They have no gifts for Herod, a breach of ancient etiquette. They want Herod to show them the new king for whom their reverence and gifts are reserved. Is it any wonder that Herod and "with him all of Jerusalem" are troubled?

The strangers know the truth. All earthly power is derived from heavenly power. The earthly king must not try to reject or thwart the plan of the heavenly King. His role is homage, prostration, and the offering of gifts. King Herod must yield to the child of the star. Oddly enough, Herod knows this is his role. So he plays it—on the outside. Inside he is filled with murderous schemes. This resistance and hypocrisy, profiled so effectively in Herod, are a real possibility when the stranger tells us our own truth, a truth that threatens the way we live.

The poem entitled "Epiphany in Doubt" restates these dynamics as it addresses the Herod in all of us. Strangers do not know the compromises we have made with our deepest truths, the silences we have agreed upon, the pacts we have made "to look the other way." Out of their own wits and in consultation with their own traditions, they discover a truth that we have long publicly proclaimed: "We eagerly await the birth of the Messiah." Naturally, they come to us for directions.

What they do not know is that we have long ago lost the map. At their request we dig it out with more fear than enthusiasm. We are then faced with the awkward dilemma of acknowledgment or deceit. Acknowledgment of this truth means "displacement," a turning around of how we think and live, putting first what we had previously abandoned. This appears to be a loss and we are tempted to lie and plot the murder of the truth. The strangers must not be heeded. Rather they must be used to kill the truth they have uncovered. This is Herod's ploy.

The poem counsels against this response. The Magi are not unwelcomed and their news is not a threat. The strangers are an opportunity to reclaim our identity. They remind us of the heart of our tradition and encourage us to rediscover our own prophecies. To heed them is to be reunited with the promises of God and to be shown the correct use of our gifts. The irony is not only that it is strangers who know the truth that will save us but also that what they tell us is our own truth that we have lost confidence in. The gifts of the Magi to Christ were gold, frankincense and myrrh. Their gift to the Herods is to lead the ones who have learned to live without promise to the child they once long awaited.

They Ride Forever

Each age reads Scripture out of its own concerns. This is doubly true of the imaginative explorations of the Magi story.

We live in a time in which our rational mind is so powerful it could trigger our extinction. No wonder the Magi become warnings to recover the child.

We live in a time in which we are sensitive to tasks of life that are built into the structure of aging. No wonder the Magi represent the stages of life.

We live in a time between times, a time of glacial shifts of consciousness. No wonder the Magi's search is hard and their find both less and more than what they expected.

We live in a time that stresses the need for personal integration and global solidarity. Now wonder the Magi symbolize a world of communion deeper than surface separations.

We live in a time in which our preoccupation with the materiality of all lives threatens to shrivel our sense of spirit. No wonder the Magi know that matter is the secret communication of spirit.

We live in a time of universal dialogue, when all traditions are learning who they are by learning who the stranger is. No wonder the Magi come from the East to bring us the news of what is being born in our midst.

To honor this way of imaginative invention I must tell you that Melchior's name was really Melissa and that it was changed not merely because of male chauvinism but because of the strange gift that she brought to the Christ child....

Chapter 6

The Close and Holy Darkness

In the distant past, in days that for the moment and perhaps forever are best forgotten, there was a preacher with the look of Christmas. He was as round as the bowl of Santa's pipe.

When he walked, he puffed; and when he sat, he plopped. He had a permanently ruddy face and his eyes always watered as if they were under the constant assault of a winter wind. Even in July he was a Christmas-card figure. But in December, with mittens and muffler, his head down, hand on hat, trudging the night snow toward the lighted church, he was the very picture of Christmas.

That is, until he preached.

Every Christmas at midnight Mass he would shun the pulpit with its upstart microphone, the suspect modern magnification of sound. Instead, he would stand directly in front of the altar—like a real priest should—and unburden himself about the birth of Christ. It was at this moment that his real gift appeared. The man had bellows for lungs.

He always began softly, his voice a low rumble like the sound of a distant train. The congregation leaned forward hoping to hear what he was saying to himself with so much earnestness. Then the rumble grew into a roar. The train was in the church. But it did not streak past and fade. It stayed and pinned people in their seats for twenty minutes.

Once the roar arrived, there was no longer any mystery about what he had been mumbling to himself. What had been a private consultation was now a public proclamation. The Christmas message that blasted into the ears of everyone with merciless repetition and hurricane force was:

"The wood of the crib is the wood of the cross."

Born to Die

This sermon was always an unprecedented hit for those who were hard of hearing. They walked into Christmas morning discarding hearing aids like crutches at Lourdes. They were convinced that full hearing had been restored to them. But for others who caught the drift of the words in the gale of sound there was considerable grumbling.

I was one of the grumblers. What was this man trying to do? Why join the crib and the cross? I was tempted to engage in an *ad hominem* attack. My suspicion was a man wrapped in blood rather than a child wrapped in swaddling clothes was the personal preference of the preacher. In his worldview happiness came and went, but suffering endured forever. Pain was the only infallible sign of the presence of God.

However, this was unfair and I was learning, ever so slowly, not to impute the worst instincts to what people considered their best efforts. So I chalked it up to a case of tunnel theological vision. In his thinking the death of Jesus redeemed us, so all aspects of the life of Christ gained significance because of their connection with his passion and death. This lopsided theology insisted that Jesus came to die, so crib and cross were a natural pairing. I disagreed with this way of thinking, but at the time it was the most generous interpretation I could come up with. And magnanimity seemed the order of the day. After all, it was Christmas.

I had forgotten about that sermon until many years later. I came across a portion of a sermon that John Donne—poet, mystic and preacher —had given on Christmas day:

The whole life Christ was a continuall Passion; others die Martyrs, but Christ was born a Martyr. He found a Golgotha (where he was crucified) even in Bethlehem, where he was born; For, to his tendernesse then, the strawes were almost as sharp as the thornes after; and the Manger as uneasie at first, as his Crosse at last. His birth and his death were but one continuall act, and his Christmas-day and his Good Friday, are but the evening and the morning of one and the same day.[1]

Christmas day and Good Friday are evening and morning of one and the same day? Maybe John Donne was a little morbid, poetically and provocatively morbid, but morbid nonetheless. Or perhaps he was in the grip of an exclusive atonement theology that could not see birth as anything but preparation for death.

But I doubted it. I was missing something.

A few years later I received a memorable Christmas card whose cover I cannot remember. It was the inside that caught my attention. The card did not open side to side but vertically, and along the edges of the interior was the outline of a starburst. Inside the starburst in faded pencil that was difficult to decipher was a long quotation attributed to Karl Rahner.

And now God says to us what he has already said to the world as a whole through his grace-filled birth: "I am there. I am with you. I am your life. I am the gloom of your daily routine. Why will you not bear it? I weep your tears—pour out yours to me, my child. I am your joy. Do not be afraid to be happy, for ever since I wept, joy is the standard of living that is really more suitable than the anxiety and grief of those who think they have no hope. I am the blind alleys of all your paths, for when you no longer know how to go any farther, then you have reached me, foolish child, though you are not aware of it. I am in your anxiety, for I have shared it by suffering it. And in doing so, I wasn't even heroic according to the wisdom of the world. I am in the prison of your finiteness, for my love has made me your prisoner. When the totals of your plans and of your life's experiences do not balance out evenly, I am the unsolved remainder. And I know

that this remainder, which makes you so frantic, is in reality my
love, that you do not understand. I am present in your needs. I have
suffered them and they are now transformed but not obliterated from
my heart.... This reality—incomprehensible wonder of my almighty
love—I have sheltered safely in the cold stable of your world. I am
there. I no longer go away from this world, even if you do not see me
now.... I am there. It is Christmas. Light the candles. They have
more right to exist than all the darkness. It is Christmas. Christmas
that lasts forever."

This talkative divine monologue gave me a clue to the dense images of the
two preachers. Their linking of death and birth and Rahner's commentary
on God's grace-filled birth as a presence to gloom, tears, anxieties, blind
alleys, unsolved remainders, and sufferings were struggling with the
same insight. They were trying to imaginatively express the depth of
the incarnation, the unalterable commitment of God to the *full* human
adventure.

This unique Christmas rhetoric—attaching death and suffering
to the birth of the Son of the Most High—plays upon three aspects of
incarnational theology. First, incarnational images and thinking have their
greatest impact when they are received by someone whose dominant way
of imagining God is as a transcendent divine being. This transcendent
divine being cares for his creation, has made a covenant with Israel, and
through his prophets often redeclares his love as a prelude to his demands.
But still, when it is all said and done, he watches from a distance. What we
yearn for and what we think will save us is his presence: "What we need
is one greater, wiser and stronger than ourselves, who can also become
little and enter into us, and then expand and raise and strengthen us; else
what does Incarnation mean?"[2] For incarnational rhetoric to be effective
the listeners or readers must sense this need at some level. Consciously

or unconsciously, they must yearn for the greater to become lesser so the lesser can become greater. In theological jargon, the summary phrase is: "God became man so that man might become God."

Secondly, although incarnation is a theological interpretation of the *whole* life of Jesus of Nazareth, it has been closely associated with his birth.[3] In popular thought incarnation was narrowed down to the moment of birth and, in some cases, to the moment of conception—Mary "bore heaven in her womb." In fact, linking the incarnation with Mary and therefore with the birth of Jesus happened both in legend and doctrine. The legend concerns an incident at the Council of Nicea. After Arius publicly declared that the Logos who became incarnate in Jesus Christ was not divine, St. Nicholas rushed up and slapped him. The council fathers could not tolerate this type of behavior so they threw Nicholas in jail. But Mary appeared in his cell and freed him. The point is that Mary knows the nature of the one she gave birth to, and she is not going to let his defender languish in prison. In the more respectable but much-less-fun world of doctrine, Mary was given the title "Theotokos," the God-Bearer. This title was conferred as a solution to a Christological debate about the relationship between the humanity and divinity in Jesus Christ. But the byproduct was that it blended with legend and held together incarnation and birth in Christian rhetoric and theology.

Thirdly, there has always been an insistence that the union of the divine and the human in Jesus Christ was not a sham. When the Son of God "took on a human nature," it was not merely clothing or posturing. One of the most powerful ways to express and communicate this insight was to stress that Jesus was no stranger to those aspects of being human that we find either disturbing or unbearable. In particular, his full humanity would be demonstrated by the fact he freely faced what we steadfastly avoid—suffering and death. The shapers of the creed felt compelled to include, "he suffered, died, and was buried." This was not just a recording

Suffering became

the symbol of the full

humanity of Christ.

of mundane historical facts but a declaration of Jesus' full humanity. He did not, as some Gnostics pictured, magically leave his body at the moment the first pain of the passion was about to begin, climb to heaven, perch on a cloud, and laugh at his tormentors. He cried out like all of us. Suffering became the symbol of the full humanity of Christ.

This, then, is the foundation for our connecting Jesus' death with his birth. It is not a morbid reminder of demise but a tribute to the reality of incarnation. At the birth of an ordinary child, it is assumed that the woes of life will inevitably arrive, so we pray for the delay of diminishment, for long life and happiness. At the birth of the Son of the Most High, there is a suspicion of favoritism. He just might be exempt, as every misguided disciple hoped. So this misconception is corrected through literary ingenuity. No sooner is he born than a hypocritical king schemes to murder him and an inn in the city of David—whose throne the angel promised he would inherit—refuses to house his birth. Threat and rejection are present at his entry into the world. The shadows at the birth of the Son of the Most High dispel the suspicion of privilege. As the rest of us, even more than the rest of us, he is born for trouble.

The animals of J. Barrie Shepherd's poem "The Silent Seers" know what the future holds:

> *Of all the witnesses*
> *around that holy manger*
> *perhaps it was the animals*
> *saw best what lay ahead*
> *for they had paced the aching roads*

slept in the wet and hungry fields
known the sharp sting of sticks
and thorns and curses
endured the constant bruise
of burdens not their own
the tendency of men to use
and then discard rather than meet
and pay the debt of gratitude.
For them the future also held
the knacker's rope, the flayer's blade
the tearing of the bodies
for the sparing of a race.
In the shadows of that stable
might it be his warmest welcome
lay within their quiet comprehending gaze?[4]

Total incarnation, unconditional and unafraid, is the secret inspiration of the strange, often dark, Christmas rhetoric of birth and death.

But the key question has been neither asked nor answered. *Why* did the Son of the Most High take on human flesh in order to die?

I wonder as I wander out under the sky,
How Jesus the Savior did come for to die,
For poor lonely people like you and like I,
I wonder as I wander out under the sky.

If Jesus had wanted for any wee thing,
A star in the sky or a bird on the wing,
Or all of God's angels in heaven to sing,
He surely could have it for he was a king.

209

I wonder as I wander out under the sky,
How Jesus the Savior did come for to die,
For poor lonely people like you and like I,
I wonder as I wander out under the sky.

The story of the incarnation, with its images and ideas, is meant to provoke this "wondering as we wander" until a breakthrough occurs. What is supposed to dawn on us, what is supposed to suffuse and shudder our entire being, what is supposed to overwhelm every resistance and pierce our hearts is classically stated in the Gospel of John: "God so loved the world that he gave his only son, that whoever believes in him should not perish but have eternal life" (Jn. 3:16). The whole point is that he came to tell "poor lonely people like you and like I" that we are loved. And the only way to get that across is to enfold us in a love so total that it includes and overcomes the power of death. It is this love that is eternal life.

Therefore, perhaps the language of death at Christmas is not as strange as it first seems. "Born to die" translates into "accompanied by love." Its ultimate purpose is to show the nonabandoning presence of God. God does not let go of the human person. Although this rhetoric is meant to surprise and stagger us, it is not completely foreign to our experience. Our love, perhaps because it is informed by divine love, also holds onto people. Especially at Christmas we remember the dead and, although we know it will cause us more pain than pleasure, we cultivate their presence. We refuse to allow death any sovereignty. The birth of Christ proclaims that love rules. Perhaps that is why ghosts and Christmas go together. Not those who haunt Scrooge, clanging about with chains and threats and pushing for repentance, but the gentle, unobtrusive spirits of people who have celebrated with us and who now are gone, the spirits of people sustained by love and therefore never far from where love is.

At Christmas the missing return. I am not sure why. If memories and unseen presences followed the liturgical calendar, their scheduled visits would be at Easter. After all, this is when death is revealed as empty, unable to entomb the elusive human spirit. But at Easter those who have passed through death seem to be in the far reaches of God, consigned to glory. However, at Christmas they seem to roam about the close reaches of God, bumping into the earthbound. Maybe it is the migration pattern of the spirit world. They winter on earth.

Or perhaps it is us, our openness, our perceptions, our willingness to entertain more and more of reality. Perhaps at Christmas we pause long enough to allow them entry into our harried hearts. I once read about a man who was sitting quietly in his chair on Christmas Eve remembering all the people who had once celebrated Christmas with him but who now were gone. His young son, around seven, entered the room and asked him, "Daddy, why are you crying?"

"Oh," said the father, "I must have something in my eye."

These words instantly triggered a memory from his own childhood. At a distant Christmas he had walked into a room and saw his aunt with tears in her eyes. "Why are you crying, Aunt Jane?" he had asked.

"Oh," she said, "I must have something in my eye."

What we have in our Christmas eyes are images of the physically missing. These images are sharp, vivid, living—conveying a strong sense of the person. We do not need the framed photos on the dresser to remind us. Yet all the time we know they are not here the way they once were. What is in our eye is:

My grandfather, at the end of a long Christmas table, sitting behind
    a plate of food, topped by a turkey leg;
My grandmother standing during grace, a sentinel over the food;
Len's father looking up from his bridge game;
Marian smiling, but not talking;

The glasses sliding down Rocco's nose;

Donald rotating that whatchamacallit in the bowl of his pipe;

Leo telling me about the time his hands were frozen and the buxom
    farm lady who…;

Moss, white hair and stomach extended, laughing like Santa Claus
    wished he could;

Ma pouring hot tea in the saucer and cooling it with her breath;

Evelyn's eye drooping as she worries about where her son should go
    to school.

And more. Ghosts travel together.

Of course, some stay for a longer period of time. They feel at home, and we feed them every Christmas delicacy from the memory of our love and friendship. Bill need not knock. The door is always open.

Bill

In the middle of every December for the last ten years, I would arrive at Bill's place around four-thirty in the afternoon. During those ten years Bill's place shifted twice, from the second floor of a two flat to the third floor of a three flat. But the opening ritual remained the same, a handshake and an offer.

"Would you like a drink?"

"If you would be having one yourself," I would say in my mock Irish accent.

"To keep you company," he would say, not attempting any accent.

We would sink into the most comfortable chairs of his living room. The glasses would be raised to Christmas.

"Should I put it on?"

"I didn't come all this way just to talk to you."

Bill would laugh and pull from his record collection an old, frayed, cardboard jacket. He would carefully tip it and the record inside would slide out. It was unscratched. Bill always held it smudgeproof, fingertips around the outer rim, and unerringly settled it on the nub of the turntable. Bill's fastidiousness is legend. The needle, a feather's weight, descended on the grooves.

All this care was the secular way we genuflected and bowed. The voice on the record and what it said was our shared sacred. It was not a typical Christmas custom. It bypassed family, church, and the exchange of gifts. But it was effective. It had stirred the spirit of Christmas in us in the past. There was no reason to think that it would not repeat its magic. All that was needed was to lean back, expose our winter souls, and let the words carry us away.

The words began:

> One Christmas was so much like another,
> in those years around the sea-town corner now
> and out of all sound except the distant speaking
> of the voices I sometimes hear a moment before sleep,
> that I can never remember whether it snowed
> for six days and six nights when I was twelve
> or whether it snowed for twelve days and
> twelve nights when I was six.

Twenty minutes later the sonorous voice of Dylan Thomas had treated us to the adventures of *A Child's Christmas in Wales*. The story did not end but, like the child himself, drifted off.

> Looking through my bedroom window, out into
> the moonlit and the unending smoke colored snow,
> I could see the lights in the windows

of all the other houses on our hill and hear
the music rising from them up the long, steadily
falling night. I turned the gas down, I got
into bed. I said some words to the close and
holy darkness, and then I slept.

Rules have a way of growing up around traditions blessed with the burden of bearing the spirit. They are meant to protect the power of the tradition, to insure its vitality. So around our brief ceremony there developed, by mutual consent yet almost without our noticing it, a number of prohibitions. It could not take place too early in December. It had to be within two weeks of the twenty-fifth, and of course under no circumstances could it be delayed until after Christmas. It was followed by dinner, but not a movie that might clutter our minds with alien images. During the recording there was often laughter, but never commentary. Solitary appreciation now, conversation later.

So it went, every year for ten years. Until in early December of 1988, just after we had been on the phone setting up a date for our Christmas ritual, Bill's left arm shook and flailed about. Within three days the doctors had diagnosed a brain tumor. Within ten days Bill had brain surgery. Over the next two years he had three more operations and two procedures ominously called a "gamma knife." There was a break in our Christmas tradition in '88. We picked it up again in '89 and '90. In the middle of December of 1991, I sat down in the late afternoon and read a copy of Dylan Thomas' *A Child's Christmas in Wales*. Although I did not have the record, I heard the lilt and rhythm of Thomas' voice in my mind. Also, every so often, in my mind, I heard Bill laugh, in particular, at one of his favorite lines about Thomas' aunt who "alas, was no longer whinnying with us." Neither was Bill. He had died on October 26.

At the funeral Jerry Egan gave a wonderful homily. It caught the humor, quirks and wisdom that Bill was famous for. However, everybody in the church could have added an anecdote. Most of the stories would be about Bill's wit and personality. But our friendship had a good deal of theological talk in it. We both read and taught theology and would often be on the phone sharing images and ideas for homilies and talks. I remember once Bill called with the opening line, "Avoid God as creator, meet him as judge. What do you think?" It alternated between theological stuff like that and jokes that could not be told in the pulpit or, for that matter, anywhere else.

Between Bill's first and second operation we saw a movie and went to a Greek restaurant for Athenian chicken. Somehow we got into a conversation we had previously avoided: how was this brain tumor sickness affecting his spirit? It was not a long conversation and it ended with Bill saying, "God is not any of the meanings, but the deeper darkness that keeps us making all the meanings. I don't want to talk about it anymore." So we didn't.

But I thought about it more. To me it said a lot about Bill and a lot about what Bill gave me. I found the positive side of it summed up in an entry of Thomas Merton's journal. It was dated two days after his enlightenment experience at a Buddhist shrine and four days before he died in Bangkok: "Suddenly there is a point where religion becomes laughable. then you decide that you are—nevertheless—religious."[5] Bill found religion laughable, was religious nevertheless, and engaged in it with great sport—the only sport Bill ever had much use for.

Religion is laughable because it reaches too far and claims too much. It glories in the little light it has but fears the great darkness that surrounds it. It pretends the starlight revelation is only in the brightness at the center and not at the impenetrable edges of night. But the always more we do not know relativizes the mind and pushes consciousness to the deeper space of spirit:

The highest image of God is the unseen behind the eyes—the blank space, the unknown, the intangible and the invisible. That is God! We have no image of that. We do not know what that is, but we have to trust it. There's no alternative.... That trust in a God whom one cannot conceive in any way is a far higher form of faith than fervent clinging to a God of whom you have a definite conception.[6]

Love resides in that blank space and also in laughter, the laughter that deflates the grandiosity and preening of the mind. Bill knew about this space, and his wild humor originated there.

Another way of saying this is that idolatry is steadfastly and thoroughly refused. Bill used to like to talk about Jesus as a Jew of the first commandment. He was centered in God and therefore decentered from himself and all other things. While he enjoyed all things, he refused to be attached to any of them. This "first commandment" approach culminated in Bill's comical yet serious theological stance of "aboutism." All religious images and ideas were "about" something. This "something" was revealed through the images, but every revelation only meant a deeper concealment. If the darkness was truly close and holy, you did not have to compulsively turn it into light. As C. S. Lewis said about the darkness of death and afterlife, "The best is perhaps what we understand least."[7] Too much of our knowing is a manic attempt to control rather than trust. This truth, when it is fully assimilated, sends some along the angry road of disillusionment. It made Bill laugh, become compassionate toward stumblers everywhere, and remain religious nevertheless.

Bill summed up his approach to his death: "I'm not afraid of dying, but I want to live." Bill was in touch with the source of vitality and so identified with it that he could not willingly forsake it. But he also knew a secret about fear. After his first operation, we went out for Chicken Vesuvio. (We were always eating some variety of garlic chicken—a boon for body, mind and spirit.) In an off-hand way he said, "It just goes to show you how insubstantial an emotion fear is, for if it had any substance at all, it would have killed me. That is how afraid I was. Imagine! Cutting a hole in someone's head!" Living in the close and holy darkness means, first of all, living and, secondly, knowing that the fear that terrorizes us cannot kill us.

I am tempted to say that every Christmas I will remember Bill. I will keep alive our mini-tradition of listening to or reading Dylan Thomas. Yet I am not very good at planning ahead. The season may be here and gone, and I will not have done this simple and important gesture. I hope not, but I cannot rule it out. However, I am more confident about another process of memory, more confident because it is a process that I have very little control over and therefore cannot mess up. It occurs spontaneously.

Living in the close

and holy darkness

means, first of all,

living, and, secondly,

knowing that

the fear that

terrorizes us

cannot kill us.

Whenever through choice or circumstances the tight grip of my mind releases and I say words to the close and holy darkness, Bill will enter my consciousness. It will happen without effort on my part. It will not be a matter of obligation or debt. He will just be there.

The Dead and the Living

At the close of James Joyce's classic short story "The Dead," Gretta tells her husband, Gabriel, of a young man who loved her so much he died for her. This stuns Gabriel (Is this the angel whose trumpet blast awakens the

217

dead?) and forces him to reflect on love and death:

> *Generous tears filled Gabriel's eyes. He had never felt like that himself toward any woman, but he knew that such a feeling must be love. The tears gathered more thickly in his eyes and in the partial darkness he imagined he saw the form of a young man standing under a dripping tree. Other forms were near. His soul had approached that region where dwell the vast hosts of the dead. He was conscious of, but could not apprehend, their wayward and flickering existence. His own identity was fading out into a grey, impalpable world: the solid world itself, which these dead had one time reared and lived in, was dissolving and dwindling. A few light taps upon the pane made him turn to the window. It had begun to snow again.... His soul swooned slowly as he heard the snow falling faintly through the universe and faintly falling, like the descent of their last end, upon all the living and the dead.*[8]

We have another man with something in his eye that causes him to pierce the partial darkness. The swooning of his soul and the dissolving of the solid world push him into a silent world of communion with the dead. Jesus tried to bridge the gulf between the unjust and the just by suggesting a common sun shone upon them and a common rain fell upon them. Is it so different to bridge the gulf between the living and the dead by suggesting a common snow falls faintly on them both?

I have always fancied this border area between the "solid world" and "grey, impalpable world" to be the spiritual situation of Mary Magdalene in the resurrection story in the Gospel of John (Jn. 20:1–18). "On the first day of the week, while it was still dark," Mary goes to the tomb, finds it empty, and in a panic runs to Peter and the beloved disciple and cries out, "They have taken the Lord out of the tomb and we do not where they have laid him." She desperately wants the *dead* body of Jesus. She is frantic when she cannot find it and blames "them" for having taken it away. She weeps, not rejoices, outside the empty tomb. When the risen Jesus asks her, "Woman, why are you weeping? Whom are you looking for?" she thinks he is the gardener and, unknowingly, voices the full irony. "Sir, if you have carried him away (and, of course, that is precisely what has happened) tell me where you have laid him and I will take him away." Mary is faced with the living presence of Christ, whom she does not recognize, because she is fixated on a body she can carry away. When the risen Christ speaks her name and she recognizes him as the Rabbi, his bodily, pre-Easter title, she immediately goes to embrace him. This woman wants a body to touch, dead or living. Jesus refuses this way of relating to him. The time of physical embrace is over: "Do not cling to me."

A sage once quipped, "The most amazing thing is that although everybody knows everybody dies, we do not think *we* will." There is a double edge to this remark. One edge is our consummate skill at avoiding and denying physical death. The second edge is that perhaps our sense that *we* will not die is not delusionary. The story of the risen Lord and Magdalene walks along both these edges. The risen Jesus does not deny physical death. What he was is dead, and his new presence is not capable of being held the way his old presence was. On the other hand, he does not honor Mary's request for a dead body. She thinks that if she had that she would have Jesus. She is not only looking for him in the wrong place, the tomb, she is looking for him in the wrong form, a separate individual body. Jesus tries to redirect her search by assuring her of his real yet different presence in the enigmatic command, "Go to my brothers and tell them, 'I am ascending to my Father and your Father, to my God and your God.'" Whoever he is, he has not been lost through the experience of death. Rather there is a new presence mediated through a common God and Father and symbolized by the ascension.

The ascension in the Gospel of John functions differently from the way it does in Luke's Gospel and the Acts of the Apostles. In Luke it signals the end of the life of Jesus and the beginning of the life of the church. In the more mystical John it signals the risen Lord's power to be with God and with his brothers and sisters simultaneously. He is going to his Father and their Father, to his God and their God. This going to God is not a going away from them but a coming and staying with them in a new way. This new way is symbolized by how Jesus encounters them. Even though the doors are locked, Jesus appears in their midst. His new presence is not bound by physical limitation and, as Thomas finds out, not properly known by physical inspection. But it is a real presence whose opening greeting is "Peace," the restoration of relationships.

What I love about Magdalene is she does not give up easily. She wants something to hold. At this stage the real world for her is constituted by touch. Is this not true of all of us? I remember a man who had recently lost his wife. He was both a strong believer in afterlife and realistic about loss and getting on with "it." But one time he said, with great sadness in his voice, "You know, Jack, sometimes you gotta feel flesh." We "gotta feel flesh" most of the time. For us flesh is the real substantial world, and without it our sense of reality, in Joyce's words, "dissolves and dwindles." We ache to hold the ones we love and press their presence into our own. Or just to see them with our eyes and hear them with our ears. We are assured by solid flesh, and when it is missing our perception of loss is so overwhelming that we cry out, "I would do anything to have my loved one back." It is at this moment that we are closest to God, whose gathering nature cannot abide loss.

Yet we are told not to cling. If this is only a brutal reminder of loss, it is unnecessarily cruel. But in the spiritual life every negation has a positive side, every turning away is a turning toward. Not clinging is the first step in the redirection of consciousness. It will not take the tears from our eyes, but it may allow us to see through the tears into the darkness. Reality may be more than we know: "Other forms were near." William Shannon tries to point out this possibility to a woman who has recently lost her sister:

> *I hope you have been able to come to grips a bit more with your feeling about your sister's death. I realize how very hard this is for you. You need to keep reflecting on the fact that, while in one sense death separates us from the loved ones, in another and more ultimate sense it deepens our spiritual union with them. When there is only that, then that becomes most important. And of course it should really be most important at all times. We are one with one another, because whatever of us there is that is really worthwhile is from God and in God. And that is something that death does not and cannot change—though it appears to do so, since we are so accustomed to think of a person solely in terms of her empirical ego. Death is the end of the empirical ego, but not of the person. We are all eternally one in the love of God.*[9]

What is outrageous in this suggestion is that we may have more intimacy with people when they are dead than we do when they are alive. It is one thing to say the person is with God, and we see it as God's gain and our loss. It is quite another thing to say that they are also intimately present to us. Not lost, but so close we cannot see them. Augustine said that God was more intimate to him than he was to himself. If the people we love and who have died are in God, then perhaps they are more intimate to us than we know: "Go tell my brothers and sister, 'I am ascending to my Father and Your Father, my God and your God.'"

If the dead are so close, perhaps there are signs of their presence?

Signs

I remember many years ago a young man came to see me. His wife had died in childbirth. There was a mistake in the medication and she had a stroke. He was suing the doctor for ten million dollars, "but I don't care about the money. I just want him to hurt." His every word carried pain and grief. I still remember what he said and what he asked: "You know my daughter's birth day will always be my wife's death day. How will I ever get over it? You know what I do? My wife played the piano, and we made audio tapes. I play them again and again. But I don't listen to the music. In between pieces she would move on the bench and her clothes would rustle. Then before she would begin a new piece she would clear her throat. That's the part I play over and over again. I'm clinging to her clearing her throat. I want a sign from her that she is okay. That's what I want. What I want to know from you, and I should tell you that it was my mother who suggested that I see you, is will I get the sign?"

I told him that in one way he already had a sign. It was his love that was larger than the loss, that refused its finality. This love was not his alone but was influenced by a larger reality of Love that held all things both in change and everlastingness. His wife was still alive in that Love and so was he and so was his daughter. True, they were separated, but because they lived by the power of the same Love they were still, in ways more subtle than flesh, in union. I had not read Shannon's letter at that time, but a similar instinct was at work.

The man said that wasn't enough. He wanted a sign from beyond. He had had a number of mystical experiences, and he sensed that this was possible. If he had a sign, he would let her go and be in peace.

I said I hoped that would be the case. But even if nothing happened, he should know that to belong to a religious tradition means that we share and make our own the special experiences of other people. Many in our tradition have experienced a love that is stronger than death and have told us of its infinite yet mysterious care. We hold on to this testimony even though at any given moment we may not have all the signs we want to assure us. We must take heart from others when our own heart is sad. I was trying to bring forth the strength of traditional faith to bolster the weakness of contemporary experience.

I hope what I said and how I said it was less preachy than this summary makes it sound, but the man having none of it. He said that made sense, but it wasn't enough. He thanked me and left. I felt that I provided little consolation and even less help—a not untypical evaluation in the day-in-day-out life of a grief minister.

I mentioned this meeting to a friend who is very knowledgeable in religion and spirituality. He casually said, "Of course he will get a sign."

"Because he wants it?" I said.

"Partly. That opens him. Something will happen, and he will see it as a sign. It will be coincidence to everyone else but revelation to him."

I had read about these types of signs and the power they held for people. A famous example is from Viktor Frankl. At the time of this experience he was a prisoner at Auschwitz:

> Another time we were at work in a trench. The dawn was grey around us; grey was the sky above; grey the snow in the pale light of dawn; grey the rags in which my fellow prisoners were clad, and grey their faces. I was again conversing silently with my wife, or perhaps I was struggling to find the reason for my sufferings, my slow dying. In a last violent protest against the hopelessness of imminent death, I sensed my spirit piercing through the enveloping gloom. I felt it transcend that hopeless, meaningless world, and from somewhere I heard a victorious "yes" in the answer to my question of the existence of an ultimate purpose. At that moment a light was lit in a distant farmhouse, which stood on the horizon as if painted there, in the midst of the miserable

*grey of a dawning morning in Bavaria. "Et lux in tenebris lucet"—
and the light shineth in the darkness. For hours I stood hacking at
the icy ground. The guard passed by, insulting me, and once again
I communed with my beloved. More and more I felt that she was
present, that she was with me; I had the feeling that I was able to
touch her, able to stretch out my hand and grasp hers. The feeling was
very strong that she was there. Then, at that very moment, a bird flew
down silently and perched just in front of me, on the heap of soil which
I had dug up from the ditch, and looked steadily at me.*[10]

In the pain of his own suffering and the loss of his wife Frankl searches for
a sign. A light shines in the darkness and a bird lands on the earth he had
dug up. These happenings are to him revelations. He senses the invisible
presence of his wife and his spirit is renewed. She cleared her throat and
the sound opened his heart.

Ram Dass tells a similar story about his mother's funeral:

*For forty-four years my mother and father on their anniversary had
exchanged, along with gifts, one red rose that was a token of their love
for one another. At the temple the casket was covered with a blanket
of roses. As the casket was wheeled out of the temple, it came by the
first pew. In the first pew were seated my father, at the time a mid-
sixties, Boston Republican lawyer, ex-president of a railroad, very
conservative; my oldest brother, a stockbroker-lawyer; my middle
brother, also a lawyer, but one who was having spiritual experiences;
me; and sisters-in-law. As the coffin went by the first pew, one rose
from the blanket of roses fell at the feet of my father. All of us in
the pew looked at the rose. We all knew the story of the exchange
of one rose, but of course nobody said anything. As we left the pew,
my father picked up the rose and was holding it as we sat in the*

limousine. Finally, my brother said, "She sent you a last message," and everybody in the car at that moment agreed. Everybody said, "Yes!" The emotion of the moment sanctioned an acceptance of a reality totally alien to at least three members of the group.[11]

Perhaps the boundary between this life and the next is more permeable than many think. There are signs. People find them in the ordinary and in the extraordinary. They are open to argument and refutation, but their impact on the ones who receive them can only be welcomed. They confirm our deepest yet frailest hope: our love for one another that says "Thou, thou shalt not die"[12] is not groundless.

C. S. Lewis moves beyond signs into direct communing. His reflections are both skeptical and stimulating:

I said, several notebooks ago, that even if I got what seemed like an assurance of H's presence, I wouldn't believe it. Easier said than done. Even now, though, I won't treat anything of that sort as evidence. It's the quality of last night's experience—not what it proves but what it was—that makes it worth putting down. It was quite incredibly unemotional. Just the impression of her mind momentarily facing my own. Mind, not "soul" as we tend to think of soul. Certainly the reverse of what is called "soulful." Not at all like a rapturous reunion of lovers. Much more like getting a telephone call or a wire from her about some practical arrangement. Not that there was any "message"—just intelligence and attention. No sense of joy or sorrow. No love even, in our ordinary sense. No un-love. I have never in any mood imagined the dead as being so—well, so business-like— yet there was an extreme and cheerful intimacy.... It wouldn't be very like what people usually mean when they use such words as "spiritual" or "mystical" or "holy." It would, if I have had a glimpse,

be—well, I'm almost scared at the adjectives I'd have to use. Brisk?
cheerful? keen? alert? intense? wide-awake? Above all, solid. Utterly
reliable. Firm. There is no nonsense about the dead.[13]

This may be a brush with the other dimension, an expansion of consciousness that momentarily communed with the spirit world. However, there is another way to envision encountering the living ones whom we, in our blindness, call the dead. We do not keep an eye open for accidental signs or an ear alert for night communiqués. Rather we go out and meet them where they are living. I think I know one of the places Margie lives.

Margie

"Jack, isn't it awful?" It was Margie on the phone, and those were her first words. Those were always her first words.

"What's awful?" I shot back.

"We have to help them."

"Who is 'them?'" Unfortunately, I knew who "we" were.

Although the names of the "it" and "them" changed, the scenario remained the same. The "it" was some oppression, some injustice, some domination of one person or group by another. The "them" were people in trouble. If there was a person in trouble anywhere on the globe, Margie awoke in the morning aware of it. She lived without anesthesia. She took in the pain of the world, not out of guilt or obligation but just because it was there and someone needed to say, "No Way!" When she died, there was a big argument about just how old she was. The correct answer was ageless.

Every Christmas she would come over to Jack and Rita Troccoli's and we would eat dinner and exchange gifts. Margie would always receive the largest purse that could be found or a flight bag with the most pockets. They would be worn out within the year. One year she gave Rita and Jack a leather-bound parchment with these words written in ink:

> *You who would walk on water must know how seabirds are not*
> *takers (except for meager sustenance) that they will not*
>
> *betray you and how the non-calculating Christ walked there*
> *teaching us how water holds not footprints*
> *so you cannot leave your mark*
>
> *the water-walker has no public life no secret life except*
> *a deep remembering of One Who stored up nothing in barns*
> *and Who never said "pay what thou owest" to any person*
> *though everyone of us are debtors*
> *(he having loved the whole world)*
>
> *which is to say love is the mystery that makes the comfortable*
> *unsure and if you need to see your footprints perhaps*
>
> *there is not enough of you that loves and therefore risks*
> *for just about every lover walks on water*

Margie used to give a talk on the burden of knowing. She knew many things, but more than anything else she knew that "love is the mystery that makes the comfortable unsure."

Margie loved to tell the story about a talk she gave to a group of women. Margie drew stick figures on the board that represented various styles of relationship. One pair of figures were grossly mismatched. The first one towered above the second and glared down at it. Although it was a simple drawing, it expressed a whole world that many people knew only too well. After the talk a woman who did not speak English came up to

227

Love is

the mystery

that makes the

comfortable

unsure.

Margie and pounded on the board, hitting the lower figure with her fist and shouting, "Me! Me! Me!"

I was in a small group where Margie told that story. One of the members said something to the effect of, "Well and good. But what if she gets out of the relationship. Where will she go? What will she do?" Margie was on the edge of her chair, her arms were out in front of her, her hands parallel to each other like they were gripping some large object. I suspect the man's head. She was about to attack, but she didn't. Instead, she slid back into the chair, did not talk for a moment, and then in a tired voice spelled out what to her was so obvious. I don't remember the exact words, but I cannot forget the drift: "Wherever there is suffering and domination, you break it. Sure you find yourself out in the dark. The problem is you've gotten used to the sin, you've gotten comfortable being a slave. Oppression is a habit. Whether you are on the top or the bottom, it doesn't make any difference. You're part of it, and part of breaking it is not knowing what to do next."

That was the close and holy darkness Margie knew, the darkness that we walk into when we walk away from the comfortable forms of alienation. If we wait for the new future before we break with the old past, we will never move. We will have to brave the darkness, even trust it, if we are to find a better way. Although Margie stressed that this type of darkness happens when we break from slavery and have not yet reached the promised land, Alan Jones describes the same experience more positively as the darkness between dreams:

Dreaming is essential for our existence. It holds life together by a series
of images and pictures. We need to dream if life is to be worth living.
From time to time, however, something wakes us up. Much to our
consternation we find ourselves in a deep and impenetrable darkness.
There is no light, no dream to hold life together. The bottom falls out
of everything. In our panic we try to go back to sleep to recapture the
old dream. The spiritual masters suggest that this moment of panic
is a thing to hold on to and treasure. The time "between dreams" is a
place to stay and wait in the darkness so that a new and larger dream
has the chance to emerge. It is only in the waiting that the horizons
of our dreaming can explode and expand. The new dream will make
new space for us and send our lives in a new direction.[14]

Margie kept waking people up into darkness and telling them that it was better than that old dream that straightjacketed themselves and others. "Nothing wrong with darkness," would be how I would paraphrase one of her messages. "Better than sunny sin."

This is the effect Margie had on many people. She was a wide-awake woman in a world gone to sleep, and when you were with her she shook you until you saw what she did. I chanced upon a poem by Denise Levertov called "St. Peter and the Angel." It is a reflection on a story from the Acts of the Apostles about an angel breaking Peter out of jail. This gave me another image for Margie's impact on people. The poem could have been entitled "St. Peter and Margie":

Delivered out of raw continual pain,
smell of darkness, groans of those others
to whom he was chained—

unchained, and led
past the sleepers,
door after door silently opening—
out!

    And along a long street's
majestic emptiness under the moon:

one hand on the angel's shoulder, one
feeling the air before him,
eyes open but fixed...

And not till he saw the angel had left him,
alone and free to resume
the ecstatic, dangerous, wearisome roads of
what he still had to do,
not till then did he recognize
this was no dream. More frightening
than arrest, than being chained to his warders:
he could hear his own footsteps suddenly.
Had the angel's feet
made any sound? He could not recall.
No one had missed him, no one was in pursuit.
He himself must be
the key, now, to the next door,
the next terrors of freedom and joy.[15]

Margie broke many people out of jail and pointed to "the next door, the terrors of freedom and joy." A dark future of freedom was always the result of breaking out of imprisonment.

One Christmas Margie gave me two shirts in two separate boxes. She handed me the first box and waited for me to open it. Inside was a steel blue shirt with epaulets on the shoulders. "There," she said, "when you wear that, you'll look like a revolutionary." It is the closest I'll ever get, I thought. Then she handed me the other box and said, "It's a shirt for the beach. You don't have to open it." Ah, Christmas gifts as revelation. Another time she gave me an award she had been given. It is a bronze plaque of a butterfly. Fidel Castro had given it to her in appreciation for all her work with the poor women of Latin America. I have it on the wall in my office. It floats above my work, way above.

But I know what Margie gave me, what she gave everybody—the mystery of love that makes the comfortable uneasy. And at Christmas, or any time of the year, I know where to find her. It will not be in remembering her infinitely protesting spirit or in that great laugh deeper than all the fight that was in her. I will find her where she lived once and lives still—in the darkness when I turn, right outside the prison door when I take the next step into the terrors of freedom and joy.

Why Do You Seek the Living among the Dead?

"Why do you seek the living among the dead?" is the question the angel asks the women who come to the tomb of Jesus. Although the question is asked in Luke's account of the rise of Easter faith, it is a puzzlement that pervades all four Gospels. The question is a profound confrontation to the expectation of the disciples. They think the dead are in tombs. The angel slyly implies that what is dead is in tombs but you are looking for (the person of) Jesus, are you not? In that case, you are in the wrong place. The job description of angels is (1) to make God's plan known and (2) to help humans cooperate with that plan. The infancy narratives of Matthew and Luke are thick with angels who are giving out complex sets of instructions and commands. However, the angel of the resurrection begins with a simple, "Not here, and why did you ever think he would be?"

Then where? If not in the tomb, then where is Jesus? Mark's angel (or young man) says he has gone before them into Galilee. Galilee is the region of mission. It seems he has started his preaching and teaching all over again, and if they wish to encounter him they will have to join the enterprise, just like the first time. Matthew's angel, who is sitting on the rock that sealed the tomb, says that Jesus will meet them on the mountain in Galilee. This is the mountain of the Sermon of the Mount. If they wish to encounter him, they must begin to live those teachings. If they do, they will meet him in that enterprise, just like the first time. As we discussed, John has Jesus simultaneously at the right hand of the Father and in the midst of his disciples. What Jesus tells the disciples finishes the conversation he began with Magdalene. He tells them where they can find him.

"Peace," says the suddenly appearing Jesus. This word denotes the restoration of relationships and is an opening greeting that is needed, for Jesus is reunited with followers who did not follow him. The disciples did not pass the test; they succumbed to temptation. They abandoned him before the crucifixion and so, in John's symbolic account, missed the climactic moment of revelation—Jesus' hour, the reason he came into the world, the event that glorified his Father's name. So Jesus shows them what they missed—his hands and his side. The story says they rejoice at this sight. I suppose this means they received the revelation of the pierced one. Pierced hands and side are an evocative symbol that can be developed in many ways. But no matter how it is interpreted, it must be the natural lead-in to the peculiar commission Jesus breathes on his friends: "As the Father has sent me, even so I send you." This is the identity of the person who cannot be found in the tomb. He is a mission who commissions. This is the identity of us all. Human life is not a static breathing for a while, which then stops. Human life is breathing spirit into the world that, in turn, encourages others to breathe spirit into the world. Death has no dominion over this process of breathing in and breathing out: "And when he had said this, he breathed on them and said, 'Receive the Holy Spirit.'" Every person is suffused by the Holy Spirit, and therefore every person can give that spirit away. Said another way, every person releases a characteristic power into the world. This power is both from the person and from God, and it is our ultimate identity. We are a life-giving spirit in the flesh and we are a life-giving spirit out of the flesh. Perhaps what the disciples see in his wounds are openings into the power of his spirit?

Death has no dominion over this process of breathing in and breathing out.

What is Jesus' characteristic power? When people have his spirit what do they do? "If you forgive the sins of any, they are forgiven; if you retain the sins of any, they are retained." When we hear this, we may think of ecclesiastical power and the sacrament of reconciliation (especially if you are Catholic). But it is primarily a statement

of personal power, summarizing the tremendous freedom that Jesus has unleashed into the world. If we insist on remembering and dwelling on the sins of others, then we keep them in those sins. We make it impossible for them to change. But if we release our hold on those sins, they are forgiven and a new person emerges. Jesus is a transcendent freedom who has the power to break the bonds that enslave us to our wrongdoings. This is where he lives, not in a tomb but where people are poised to either create a new reconciliation or fall back into an old alienation. It should be easy to guess which option Jesus prefers. He came to the ones who abandoned him with the offer of peace.

In fact, that is where we will find all our "lost" loved ones. I suppose we could sit and wait and hope they will appear, and then be depressed when they do not or elated at an ambiguous happening that we interpret as communication. But is not this too static a view of them as persons? Did they not pour themselves into life? Did they not shape the infinite energy of God into a peculiar and distinctive power? Did they not breathe on us this spirit and send us out? We know where they live. They live where they have always lived. If it was in the spirit of welcome, then welcome a person and you will find the one you love. If it was in the spirit of service, then serve and meet your loved one's power again. If it was in the spirit of political change, then join efforts with people and see if your loved one does not appear. We meet the ones we can no longer touch by placing ourselves in situations where their spirits still flourish. There is no indication that Magdalene ever returned to the tomb again. Why seek the living among the dead?

Christmas Peace

The Christmas season is notorious for depression and sadness. Preachers try to tone down their rhetoric of "peace, joy, love" because these commanded feelings can be the good news background for guilt. We are supposed to be soaring and we are crashing. We are out of sync with the season and no amount of encouragement can turn us around. Feelings do not respond to determination and will power. It is not a matter of trying harder to be happy. Some psychological theories hold that feelings are cognitive-dependent. How we see things influences how we feel. If we can change the way we see things, a new flood of feelings will accompany the new perceptions. This is not a cure-all for holiday blues, but it is a direction that should be taken seriously.

Christmas sadness is often connected with obsessing on the loss of people we love. We miss them so much and are so fixated on what is gone that all we can see is the gardener. They were so much a part of us that to lose them is to lose ourselves. The more we remember them as physically missing, the more we feel isolated and alone. I suspect that this will forever be the case with incarnate beings. We will never bypass the weeping Magdalene who cannot find the body. But perhaps we could also join her in her mission of proclaiming a new presence? If we seek out the life-giving spirit of the ones we love, the same life-giving spirit that flowed from them while they were in the flesh, we may find a new presence awaiting us. If we saw it this way and acted in this way, the sadness would undoubtedly still be there, but it might become gentle, sadness that does not crush but is borne lightly, borne by human spirits that have learned to ride time.

In other words, we counter Christmas sadness with Christmas peace. In Luke's story after the angel announces the birth of the Messiah, she is joined by a multitude of the heavenly hosts singing, "Glory to God in the highest and peace on earth to people on whom his favor rests." This is a difficult verse to translate.[16] But one of its meanings could be that it is the good pleasure of the transcendent divine to reconcile all people who are estranged from one another. Put simply, what makes God happy is people together. We often wish people the peace of Christmas, but we may not have a clear notion of what we extending. Peace can mean an inner calm that fends off anxiety for the moment. It can also mean an ultimate assurance of well-being despite proximate troubles and tribulations. Christmas peace certainly plays upon these two meanings, and we see them as very desirable and hope that all people find inner tranquility.

However, the primary thrust of peace is reconciliation between peoples. Therefore, to extend Christmas peace is to actively take down the barriers between yourself and another person. We do not know what barriers exist for those who, from our limited earthly perspective, we call the "dead." But on this side of the divide the barrier is clear. We have not actively engaged the spirit they breathed on us. When we do, our physical loss will be tempered by spiritual presence. Christmas peace is an action we engage in to reconcile ourselves with the spirit of those whose love is longing to be carried on. When we do this, we will learn the truth of the heavenly song. The heart of reality takes deep pleasure in restoring all relationships.

This Christmas I will play or read Dylan Thomas's *A Child's Christmas in Wales*. I know I will not get through it without experiencing that explosion of emptiness we call loss. But if I train my spirit to stop my devouring and controlling mind, to relate humbly to the spawn of ideas in my speaking and teaching, I will come to a place so dark that only trust is possible, the close and holy darkness where Bill lives.

I will also be in Jack and Rita's living room and for a moment my mind will slip. I will be waiting for Margie to enter laughing, package-laden, with stories about traffic and getting lost. Then I will pull out of it and the emptiness will be so draining I will grip the arm of the chair. I do not know if I am trying to steady myself or just be reassured by something solid. But if I walk away from some comfortable alienation and for once do not consider what comes next, if I just stand firm in the conviction that something wrong is over, then in that darkness before the next step, in the close and holy darkness, I will meet her.

Such is the starlight way of sadness and presence, the way of spirits in the flesh and out of the flesh, the way of those who attend the birth of the One who is born to die.

Chapter 7

The Man Who Was a Lamp

Legend says,
the cave of Christmas
where the child of light
burns in the darkness
is hidden
in the center of the earth.

Access is not easy.
You cannot just amble to a mantle,
note the craft of the crib child,
and return to the party for more eggnog.
You may see a figurine in this way,
but you will not find the child of light.
The center of the earth is not the surface.
You must journey
and, wayfarer,
you need a guide.

Even the Wise Men had to risk
the treacherous courts of Herod
to consult the map of Scripture.
They knew that a star, no matter how bright,
could not take them all the way.
It is true
that sometimes angels hover in the sky
and sing directions,

237

but they cannot be counted on
to appear.
Besides, you are not one
to keep watch over a flock by night.

There is another pointer of the way,
a map of a man,
who when you try to read him,
reads you.
Unexpected angels are pussycats
next to this lion,
a roar that once overrode Judea.
You may not heed
but you will hear
his insistent,
intruding,
unsoothing voice.
Some say this thunder is because his father
stumbled mute from the Holy of Holies,
tongue tied by an angel who was peeved
by the old man's stubborn allegiance to biological laws.
The priest was silenced in the temple
    because he thought flesh could stop God.
The son of the priest shouted in the wilderness
    because he feared God would stop flesh.
His open mouth was an open warning.

His name is John,
a man who was a lamp,
    at least that is what Jesus said,

"a burning and shining lamp."
The implication is clear:
The lamp is a torch through the darkness
to find the Light of the World.
As the lamp comes closer to the Light,
its radiance is overwhelmed.
It is in the presence of a stronger shining.
It decreases as the Light increases.
Yet there is no comparison.
The child cannot be found by competition.
The lamp and the Light meet
in the mystery of communion.
The two become one
while remaining two.
Follow John and find Jesus.
Find Jesus and find the fullness of John.

But John is not so easy to follow.
He is no toady.
He lacks servility
and does not work for pay.
In truth,
he is more guardian than guide,
more dragon at the gate than porter at the door,
more fire on the earth than lamp on a stand.
Opposite of the sought-after child in every way.
The child is round,
this one has edges;
the child nurses on virgin's milk,
this one crunches locusts;

the child is wrapped in swaddling clothes,
this one is rubbed raw by camel hair.
Yet they know each other,
even exchange smiles.
They share a mystery,
this hairy man and smooth child.

Jesus came out of John
    as surely as he came out of Mary.
John was the desert soil
    in which the flower of Jesus grew.
John was the voice in the wilderness
    who taught Jesus to hear the voice from the sky.
John would push sinners beneath the water
    and Jesus would resurrect them on the waves.
John was the fast
    who prepared for Jesus the feast.

No man ever less a shepherd than John,
    yet loved by one.

If you are surprised that Jesus came from John,
    imagine John's prophetic puzzle
when the predicted "wrath to come" came
    and said, "Let's eat!"
John expected an ax to the root of the tree
    and instead he found a gardener hoeing around it.
He dreamt of a man with a winnowing fan and a fire
    and along came a singing seed scatterer.
He welcomed wrathful verdicts,

then found a bridegroom on the bench.
When John said, "There is one among you
    Whom you do not know,"
he spoke from experience.

So from prison
John sent his disciples to Jesus.
    He will send you too.
    Despite his reputation,
    he is best at introductions.
    It is simply who he is,
    preparer, primer, pointer,
    a tongue always on the verge of exclaiming,
    "Behold!"

His question was, "Are you the One Who Is to Come
or should we look for another?"

    This arrow of a question was sent from prison
    but the bow was bent in the desert
    by "none greater born of woman"
    who was awake before the sun,
    waiting,
    watching the vipers flee before the morning
    his eyes welcomed.

    "Are you the One Who Is to Come"
    is the question of John highway,
    his road under construction,
    hammer and pick and hardhat song,

"I have leveled a mountain
and raised a valley
to make even the path of the Lord!"

You
are the mountain
his sunburnt muscles
are slamming to cracked rock.
You
are the valley
his tattooed arms
are filling with broken earth.
He will trowel you to smooth,
and when there is no impediment,
when there is nothing in you
which would cause a child to trip,
you will yearn for someone to arrive
and ask the question
that guards the cave of Christmas,
"Are you the One Who Is to Come?"
So do not go fearfully
into John's wilderness,
    beaten from civilization by others
    or driven by your own self-loathing.
Go simply because it is the abode
    of wild beasts and demons
and, given all you are,
you will most certainly feel at home.
Wrestle with the rages of the soul,
talk to the twistedness.

Try no tricks on him.
Parade no pedigree.
Who you know will not help you.
If the children of Abraham and stones
have equal standing in his eyes,
you will not impress him
with anything you pull from your wallet.

Also do not ready your brain for debate.
He is not much for talk.
He has washed his mind with sand.
Injunctions are his game.
    If you have two coats or two loaves of bread,
    share them.
    Do not bully,
    do not exploit,
    do not falsely accuse.
Do not object that these actions are
economically naive,
culturally inappropriate,
insufficiently religious.
Just do them.
Afterwards,
you will be unencumbered,
yet lacking nothing,
freer to move, to bend.
The entrance to the cave is low.

John's desert is the place between slavery and promise,
out of Egypt but not yet in the waters of the Jordan,

Your sojourn there will burn away
the last marks of the shackles
and you will stand unfettered.
You will be between the castle and the crowd,
between fine garments and reeds shaken by the wind.
You will not lord it over others
and you will not be pushed around.
Prophet?
Yes, and more.
But in the thrill of freedom
it will take you a moment to notice
what that more is.
In the emptiness of John's desert
you will find yourself waiting,
like a bowl that waits for wine,
like a flute that waits for breath,
like a sentinel that waits for the dawn.
You are a highway ready for traffic,
and here comes One
who seems also to have been waiting,
waiting for the construction to be complete.
The more is arriving,
and there is only one question,
"Are you the One Who Is to Come?"

Jesus answered,
"Go and tell John
what you see and hear."

So they did.

The disciples of John returned on the night of Herod's birthday.
The music and laughter of the celebration
twisted down the stairs to the dungeon
beneath the earth.
They talked to John through the bars.
They could barely make him out
in the shadows.

We saw a blind woman staring at her hand,
first the palm, then the back,
over and over again,
twisting it like a diamond in the sun,
weeping all the time and saying,
"I can see through tears! I can see through tears!"

We saw a lame man
bounce his granddaughter
on his knee.

We saw a leper
kiss her husband.

We saw a deaf boy
snap his fingers
next to his ear
and jump.

We saw a dead girl
wake and stretch
and eat breakfast.

The poor we saw
were not poor.

They paused.
Although there was no light in the dungeon,
there was a glow around John.
It softened the fierceness of his face
yet took no strength away.
When he had preached on the banks of the Jordan,
they could not take their eyes off his fire.
Now this new light made them look down.
    Jesus said
    we would be blest
    if these sights did not scandalize us.

John was silent.
When he spoke,
the words had no urgency.
There was no strain in his voice.
It was no longer
the voice in the wilderness.
    The guards tell me that Herod,
    panting,
    has promised Salome
    half a kingdom
    if she will dance for him.
    Surely she will ask for me
    for I am half a kingdom.
    I can denounce a king
    but I cannot enthrone one.

I can strip an idol of its power
but I cannot reveal the true God.
I can wash the soul in sand
but I cannot dress it in white.
I devour the Word of the Lord like wild honey
but I cannot lace his sandal.
I can condemn the sin
but I cannot bear it away.
Behold, the lamb of God
who takes away the sin of the world!

Yet he came to me
    to go beyond me.
He entered the water
to rise out of it.
He knew I would know him when he came
even though I did not know him before he came.
The fulfillment is always more than the promise,
but if you hunger and thirst in the promise,
you will welcome the One Who Is Not You
as All You Are,
and more.
    Go back
and tell Jesus
what you see and hear —
John,
not scandalized but fulfilled,
witness to his coming.

When you told me
what you saw and heard,
I knew who I was:
the cleanser of eyes but not the sight that fills them,
the opener of ears but not the word that thrills them.
A prophet?
Yes, and more.
Friend of the Bridegroom.
And more.
It was love in the desert and I did not know it.
It was love by the river and I did not know it.
It is love in this cave and now I know it.
Bridegroom myself!

The guards clattered down the stairs,
their impotent swords drawn.
They pushed aside the disciples
and unlocked a dungeon of light
to find John dancing,
his feet moving to the long-ago memory
of womb kicks.
Who was about to lose his head to Herod
had lost his mind to God.

The cave of Christmas
is hidden
in the center of the earth.
You will need a lamp for the journey.
A man named John
is a step ahead of you.

His torch sweeps the ground
so that you do not stumble.
He brings you,
at your own pace,
to the entrance of the cave.
His smile is complete,
perfect,
whole,
lacking nothing.

Inside
there is a sudden light,
but it does not hurt your eyes.
The darkness has been pushed back by radiance.
You feel like an underwater swimmer
who has just broken the surface of the Jordan
and is breathing in the sky.
John is gone.
Notice
from whom the light is shining,
beloved child.

Afterword – 2006 Edition

Have a Defiant Life!

The Christmas season can go wildly wrong. It can degenerate into mindless consumerism and an excess of food and drink. Instead of supporting relationships, it can be a time when relationships are under too much pressure and too many demands. We may pray for our relationships to survive Christmas more than we pray for Christmas to renew our relationships. As one cynic remarks, Christmas is the unsuccessful attempt to love all your family at the same time. We may stumble bloated and stressed from the house of Christmas to seek the shelter of a bland January.

But the Christmas season can also go stunningly right. It can bring us back to the hidden truth about ourselves. We are more than the state of our physical health and social standing. We are beloved children wrapped in swaddling clothes and laid in a manger. We are sustained by God's own being and called to body forth this transcendent love into the world. Our true names are salt of the earth and light of the world. This identity situates us in a relational flow between the Divine Source, our neighbors, the earth, and the universe. The chapters of this book, each in their own way, invite us to become conscious of this flow and defy anything that ignores or obstructs it. But this defiance should not be restricted to one month of the year. Christmas defiance is meant to unfold into a defiant life. As Karl Rahner remarked, it will be a "Christmas that lasts forever."

This defiant life, like a defiant Christmas, is neither negative nor angry. It is built on the simple recognition that our spiritual identity is the deepest truth about us and it needs to be integrated into our mental and social lives. Our mental and social lives are often out-of-sync with our love relationship with God. Therefore, we should not bow to the mental

251

habits and social arrangements that alienate us from ourselves and one another. Although alienation tries to convince us it is the inevitable way of human existence, it should be defied. This unyielding "no" should be balanced by an equally unyielding "yes." We should bring forward our love relationship with God as the pressure to bring into communion all that is alienated. Our birthright, revealed in the birth of Christ, is to be mediators of Divine Love as it transforms us and the world we live in.

However, this mission of transformation is not a romantic undertaking. It is strenuous activity accompanied by analytic and strategic thinking and acting. A great labor is involved. In the face of great labor we are always tempted to fall into a default mode and accept the present interpersonal and social arrangements as unchangeable. In an intransigent world, defiance can collapse into capitulation. Going along becomes more realistic than pushing back. The inner energy of defiance seems no match for the lethargy of the world.

This sense of how entrenched the ways of alienation are shakes our confidence. We suspect we are not up to the task. We do not have the knowledge and skills to inform interpersonal and social situations with the spiritual qualities we value. Our efforts are insufficient and ineffective. Sometimes what we do even increases alienation rather than alleviates it. The truth is we can dream more than we can execute, and this dream capacity can work against us. We become resigned to a mental and social life we know is not our true home.

Into this stalled consciousness comes John the Baptist. He is the guardian of Christmas defiance. His insistent message awakens us from sleep: "Repent!" But repentance is not taken in the conventional sense as a message for sinners. Rather repentance is the natural redoing of thought and action that must accompany the efforts of serious people to cooperate with divine creativity. It is what defiant people have to embrace in order to be effective. Whoever tries to embody transcendent love in finite forms will need to try again and again and again. We are experiments in incarnation, and the experiments are never over. John the Baptist is often portrayed as shouting. But his message is really a whisper into the deepest recesses of our soul: "Don't lose heart."

We are experiments in incarnation, and the experiments are never over.

A number of years ago, I received a teaching that is closely connected with not losing heart in the defiant life. I was giving a workshop on storytelling, and at the break a Native American woman in traditional address approached me.

"You talk a lot about power, but you don't mean power," she said.

"I don't?"

"No," she replied, and her tone let me know I was about to be taught. "Power is like a fire. It flares up and burns out."

Then she stepped back, put her arm out, and steadily drew it horizontally across my line of vision. My eyes followed the firm, slow motion of her hand and arm.

"You mean strength," she said slowly. Then she smiled.

She was right. I did mean strength. The stories I told were celebrating a steady strength, an inner rootedness and resolve that could push back at what was happening. They were tales of defiant people, persevering until life changed for the better.

The energy of a defiant life is a persevering strength. This strength is not given once and for all. It needs to be renewed, revitalized, brought back from smoldering ashes into vigorous flame. This is the spiritual role of Christmas. When we know what Christmas is meant to do, we can help Christmas do it. We can embrace the season in such a way that it is not a harried time that depletes us but an invitation into a consciousness that sustains us. The food and drink in our mouths, the sights in our eyes, the music and words in our ears, the smells in our nostrils, and the textures open to our touch seek to bring us into a peace that is an endless source of fight. When the season is working well and we are cooperating with it, it renews our soul.

So we can expect to enter December battered by the intransigent world and frustrated by our own lackluster efforts. But we can also expect to find—and every time is the first time—a light shinning in the darkness, a greenness refusing to give in to barrenness, and a love that persistently outlasts rejection. Then we will walk into January recommitted, a defiant Christmas energizing a defiant life.

Permissions

Notes

Preface: Starlight

1. Quoted in *A Christmas Sourcebook*, ed. Mary Ann Simcoe (Chicago: Liturgy Training Publications, 1984), 3.

2. Ibid.

3. *G. K. Chesterton: The Spirit of Christmas*, selected and arranged by Marie Smith (New York: Dodd, Mead & Company, 1985), 81.

4. *Hamlet*, I.i.

5. Raymond Schwager, "Christ's Death and the Prophetic Critique of Sacrifice," *Semeia* 33, 120. Emphasis mine.

6. Vaclav Havel, *Disturbing the Peace* (New York: Vintage, 1991), 181.

7. Evelyn Underhill, *Man and the Supernatural* (New York: E. P. Dutton & Co., 1929), 101.

8. Willa Cather, *Death Comes for the Archbishop* (New York: Alfred A. Knopf, 1927), 50.

9. See how Meister Eckhart develops this text in his homily for Christmas midnight Mass. *Breakthrough: Meister Eckhart's Creation Spirituality*, introduction and commentary by Matthew Fox (Garden City, N.Y.: Doubleday, 1980), 293–312.

10. Quoted in *A Christmas Sourcebook*, 13.

11. Quoted in Larry Dossey, *Recovery of Soul* (New York: Bantam, 1989), 19.

12. *Angelus Silesius: The Cherubic Wanderer*, trans. Maria L. Shrady (Mahwah, N.J.: Paulist Press, 1986), 71–72.

Chapter 1: The Soul and the Season

1. Evelyn Underhill, "The Spiritual Life," *Modern Spirituality: An Anthology*, ed. John Garvey (Springfield, Ill.: Templegate, 1985), 16.

2. See Cyprian Smith, *Meister Eckhart: The Way of Paradox* (New York: Paulist Press, 1987), 103. He develops this image in Eckhart's thought and points out that Eckhart received the image from Avicenna.

3. *The Theologica Germanica of Martin Luther*, trans. Bengt Hoffman (New York: Paulist Press, 1980), 68.

4. Quoted in *Two Suns Rising: A Collection of Sacred Writings*, ed. Jonathan Star (New York: Bantam Books, 1991), 7–8.

5. Quoted in Edward Stevens, *Spiritual Technologies* (Mahwah, N.J.: Paulist Press, 1990), 100.

6. *Theologica Germanica*, 68.

7. *The Words of Gandhi*, selected by Richard Attenborough (New York: Newmarket Press, 1982), 75.

8. For a clear discussion of the distinction between line and boundary see Ken Wilber, *No Boundaries* (Boston: Shambhala Press, 1979), 10–12.

9. Alfred North Whitehead, *Process and Reality* (New York: Free Press, 1978), 5.

10. Ibid., 5.

11. Beatrice Bruteau, "Global Spirituality and the Integration of East and West," *Cross Currents* (Summer/Fall 1985): 190.

12. Chaim Potok, *The Gift of Asher Lev* (New York: Alfred A. Knopf, 1990), 100.

13. See Peter Occhiogrosso, *Through the Labyrinth: Stories of the Search for Spiritual Transformation in Everyday Life* (New York: Viking, 1991).

14. James Hillman, *Insearch: Psychology and Religion* (New York: Chas. Scribner's Sons, 1967), 44.

15. David Toolan, *Facing West from California's Shores* (New York: Crossroad, 1989), xiii.

16. Edward Schillebeeckx, *Interim Report on "Jesus" and "Christ"* (New York: Crossroad, 1981), 50.

17. Phyllis McGinley, "The Ballad of Befana: An Epiphany Legend," *In the Spirit of Wonder*, ed. M. L. Shrady (New York: Pantheon Books, 1961).

18. John Shea, *The Hour of the Unexpected* (Valencia, Calif.: Tabor, 1977), 108.

19. Thomas Hardy, "The Oxen," in *Poems of Christmas*, ed. Myra Cohn Livingston (New York: Atheneum, 1980), 20.

20. G. K. Chesterton on Christmas pudding is not to be missed. See G. K. Chesterton, *The Spirit of Christmas*, selected and arranged by Marie Smith (New York: Dodd, Mead & Company, 1985), 21.

21. Ibid., 90.

22. *The Spirit of Christmas*, 12.

23. Herbert Richardson, *Toward An American Theology* (New York: Harper & Row, 1967), 61–70.

24. See the important distinction of belief, faith, experience, and adaptation in Ken Wilber, *A Sociable God* (Boston: Shambhala, 1984), 65–74.

25. Nicholas Lash, "On Steiner's Real Presences," *New Blackfriars* (March 1990): 110–11.

26. W. H. Auden, *For the Time Being: A Christmas Oratorio in Religious Drama 1* (New York: Living Age Books, 1957), 56.

27. Ibid., 68.

28. Galway Kinnel, "To Christ Our Lord," *The Avenue Bearing the Initial of Christ into the New World: Poems 1946–64* (Boston: Houghton Mifflin Company, 1974), 44–45.

29. Max Scheler, *Ressentiment* (Glencoe, Ill.: Free Press of Glencoe, 1961), 89.

Chapter 2: Strange Stories, Spiritual Sight, and Blurred Guides

1. This is primarily a story meant to be told and heard, not read. Treat yourself to Bob Wilhelm's fine rendition: Storyfest Journeys, 3901 Cathedral Avenue, #608-B, Washington, DC 20016.

2. For a fuller exploration of the genealogy and its meanings see Raymond Brown, *A Coming Christ in Advent* (Collegeville, Minn.: Liturgical Press, 1988).

3. Ibid.

4. Gary Zukav, *The Seat of the Soul* (New York: Simon & Schuster, 1990), 27.

5. Quoted in Larry Dossey, *Recovering the Soul: A Scientific and Spiritual Search* (New York: Bantam Books, 1989), 37.

6. Beatrice Bruteau, "The Mystical Rose," unpublished paper.

7. Beatrice Bruteau, "The Communion of Saints," to be published in *Living Prayer*}.

8. Quoted in *Weavings* 2, no. 6 (November/December 1987): 28–29.

9. Quoted in Douglas John Hall, "Theology Is an Earth Science," *Faith That Transforms* (New York: Paulist Press, 1987), 108.

10. *The Words of Gandhi*, selected by Richard Attenborough (New York: Newmarket Press, 1982).

11. Wendy Wright, "For All the Saints," *Weavings* (September/October 1988): 15.

12. Quoted in Avery Dulles, *Models of Revelation* (New York: Doubleday, 1985).

13. Evelyn Underhill, *Collected Papers of Evelyn Underhill* (London: Longmans, Green, & Co., 1946), 228.

14. Anthony de Mello, *The Song of the Bird* (Chicago: Loyola University Press, 1982), 26–27.

15. Evelyn Underhill, *Man and the Supernatural* (New York: E. P. Dutton & Co., 1929), 113.

16. See Eugene LaVerdiere, "Jesus the First-Born," *Emmanuel* 89 (1983): 546–48.

17. Robert Frost, "Kitty Hawk," *The Poetry of Robert Frost* (New York: Holt, Rinehart, and Winston, 1969).

18. Quoted as the frontispiece in Bede Griffiths, *Return to the Center* (Springfield, Ill.: Templegate, 1976).

19. There are various exercises that facilitate this process of disengaging our identity from partial aspects of our existence. See Beatrice Bruteau, "Freedom: 'If Anyone Is in Christ, That Person Is a New Creation,'" *Who Do People Say I Am?*, ed. Francis A. Eigo (Villanova, Pa.: Villanova University Press, 1980), 133–34; Ken Wilber, *No Boundary* (Boston: Shambhala, 1985), 128–29; Cyprian Smith, *Meister Eckhart: The Way of Paradox* (New York: Paulist Press, 1987), 45–48.

20. Beatrice Bruteau, "Feature Book Review," in *International Philosophical Quarterly* (Fall 1991).

21. Jane Vonnegut Yarmolinsky, *Angels without Wings* (Boston: Houghton Mifflin Company, 1987), 74,

22. G. K. Chesterton, *The Everlasting Man* (New York: Dodd, Mead & Company, 1925), 222–23.

23. Peter Occhiogrosso, *Through the Labyrinth* (New York: Viking, 1991), 19.

24. Sigrid Undset, *Christmas and Twelfth Night* (London: Longmans, Green and Co., 1932), 25–26.

25. This is the question of state-specific knowledge. Statements both oral and written, that originate in a state of spiritual consciousness need a similar state in the listener or reader in order to be interpreted properly. If that consciousness is not present, the statement is either dismissed, distorted, or kindly but wrongheadedly declared to be paradoxical. See

Charles Tart, "States of Consciousness and State-Specific Sciences," *Science* 176 (1972).

26. Eknath Easwaran, *The End of Sorrow* (Petaluma, Calif.: Nilgiri Press, 1975), 24.

27. Cullen Murphy, "Who Do Men Say That I Am," *Atlantic Monthly* (December 1986): 58.

28. I take this word "masters" to be a traditional way of referring to women and men who know both the single goal and many paths of the spiritual life, and who have attempted to "walk in the spirit." These people are able to "give away" both their knowledge and, to some extent, their experience.

29. G. K. Chesterton, "My Experience of Santa Claus," *The Tablet* 2, no. 28 (December 1974).

Chapter 3: Waking Up on Christmas Morning

1. Vatican II, Declaration on the Relation of the Church to Non-Christian Religions, Oct. 28, 1965, no. 2.

2. The reflections in this book are mostly about Christmas as a response to spiritual searching. However, the feast of Christmas is not restricted to those already seeking. It has the power to open the closed, to awaken the sleeping, to oust people out of the house of satisfaction into the desert of search. From my meditation I think the primary texts of Scripture and their development in the tradition present Christmas as a summation of Christian faith, as food for the hungry and drink for the thirsty. But the feast itself, in typical paradoxical fashion, has the power to initiate searching rather than culminate it. It can make the full hungry and the slaked thirsty.

3. See Ken Wilber, *The Sociable God* (Boston: Shambhala, 1984), 65–75.

4. Charles Tart, *Waking Up* (Boston: New Science Library, 1986), 7.

5. Thomas Merton, "Conscience of a Christian Monk," *Life and Contemplation*, tape series (Chappaqua, N.Y., Electronic Paperbacks).

6. Robert Nozick, *The Examined Life* (New York: Simon and Schuster, 1989), 55–56.

7. Ibid., 58.

8. Charles Dickens, *Sketches by Boz*, quoted in Sheila Pickles, ed., *Christmas* (New York: Harmony Books, 1989), 9.

9. For the full story see Kevin Shanley, O. Carm.,"A Moment's Peace," *Catholic Digest* (December 1989): 137–39.

10. Karl Rahner, *Theological Investigations* (New York: Seabury, 1973), 9:139.

11. Quoted in William Shannon,"Thomas Merton and the Quest for Self-Identity," *Cistercian Studies* 22 (1987): 2, 184.

12. John Updike, *Self-Consciousness* (New York: Alfred A. Knopf, 1989).

13. Quoted in Michael Gelven, *Spirit and Existence: A Philosophical Inquiry* (Notre Dame: University of Notre Dame Press, 1990), 3–21. See this book for a strong argument that the origin of the spirit is in the experience of disgust at the prospect that we are only well-developed animals.

14. Eknath Easwaran, *Original Goodness* (Petaluma, Calif.: Nilgiri Press, 1989), 13.

15. For a careful exegesis of this verse see David Noel Freedman, "What the Ass and the Ox Know—But the Scholars Don't," *Bible Review* (February 1985): 42–44.

16. Elie Wiesel, *Messengers of God* (New York: Random House, 1976), 97.

17. Bede Griffiths, *Return to the Center* (Springfield, Ill.: Templegate, 1976), 16.

18. Quoted by Richard Attenborough as the saying that stirred him to

make a film about Gandhi; *The Words of Gandhi* (New York: Newmarket Press, 1982), 7.

19. For a development of what it means to be beloved see Henri Nouwen, "Forgiveness: The Name of Love in a Wounded World," *Weavings* 7, no. 2 (March/April 1992): 6–15.

20. Stephen Levine, *Who Dies?* (New York: Doubleday, 1982), 184.

21. There are many other ways in which the child metaphor can be developed. It has evoked insights about the child's freedom from the culturally biased mind (see William Shannon, *Thomas Merton's Dark Path* [Toronto: Collins Publishers, 1987], 83); adult access to the child's wholistic appreciation of life (see Hubert Benoit, *Zen and the Psychology of Transformation* [New York: Pantheon Books, 1955], 110); the child's capacity to play as essential to every stage of life (see Rubem Alves, *Tomorrow's Child* [New York: Harper \& Row, 1972], 86); and child's sense of a transcendent self (see Ken Wilber, *No Boundary* [New York: Random House, 1979], 134).

22. See the development of child spirituality in Beatrice Bruteau, "Global Spirituality and the Integration of East and West," *Cross Currents* (Summer/Fall 1985): 190–205.

23. Beatrice Bruteau, "The Living One: Transcendent Freedom Creates the Future," *Cistercian Studies* no. 1 (1983): 56.

24. In *God Makes the Rivers to Flow: Passages for Meditation*, selected by Eknath Easwaran (Petaluma, Calif.: Nilgiri Press, 1982).

Chapter 4: Giving Birth to Christ

1. The best way to experience this story is to hear it. Robert Bela Wilhelm has it on tape: Storyfest Journeys, 3901 Cathedral Avenue, #608-B, Washington, DC 20016.

2. See Sophy Burnham, *A Book of Angels* (New York: Ballantine, 1990) and *Angel Letters* (New York: Ballantine, 1991).

3. Jean Houston, *Godseed: The Journey of Christ* (Warwick, N.Y.: Amity House, 1988), 31.

4. *Angelus Silesius: The Cherubic Wanderer*, trans. Maria L. Shrady (Mahwah, N.J.: Paulist Press, 1986), 2:102.

5. *The Poems of John of the Cross*, trans. Roy Campbell (New York: Pantheon Books, 1951), 89.

6. Beatrice Bruteau, "The Finite and the Infinite," *The Quest* (Summer 1989): 66.

7. This story is told in full in Ram Dass and Paul Gorman, *How Can I Help?* (New York: Alfred A. Knopf, 1985), 191–92.

8. Beatrice Bruteau, "Prayer: Insight and Manifestation," *Contemplative Review* (Fall 1983): 29.

9. This story was told to me during a workshop on storytelling.

10. These quotes are strung together in Patrick Bearsley, "Mary the Perfect Disciple: A Paradigm for Mariology," *Theological Studies* 41, no. 3 (September 1980): 479.

11. *Meister Eckhart* trans. Edmund Colledge and Bernard McGinn (New York: Paulist Press, 1981), sermon 22, 192.

12. See "Sermon: Jesus Entered," *Meister Eckhart: Mystic and Philosopher*, trans. with commentary by Reiner Schurmann (Bloomington: Indiana University Press, 1972), 9.

13. Caryll Houselander, *The Reed of God* (New York: Sheed & Ward, 1944), 6, emphasis mine.

14. Ibid., 3.

15. John Layard, *The Virgin Archetype* (Dallas: Spring Publications, 1977), 290–91.

16. Anthony de Mello, *One Minute Wisdom* (New York: Doubleday, 1986).

17. Quoted in Larry E. Carden, "Waiting: Spiritual Transformation and the Absence of God," *St. Luke's Journal of Theology* (June 1988): 198.

18. Quoted in Robert McAfee Brown, *Persuade Us to Rejoice: The Liberating Power of Fiction* (Louisville, Ky.: Westminster/John Knox Press, 1992).

19. See Terrence Mullins, "New Testament Commission Forms, Especially in Luke-Acts," *Journal of Biblical Literature* 95, no. 4 (1976): 603–14. For a different opinion, which stresses that this passage is more basically a birth announcement, see Raymond Brown, "Gospel Infancy: Narrative Research from 1976 to 1986: Part II (Luke)," *Catholic Biblical Quarterly* 48: 663.

20. Madeleine L'Engle, *The Glorious Impossible* (New York: Simon & Schuster, 1990).

21. Huston Smith, *Forgotten Truth* (New York: Harper & Row, 1976), 74–75.

22. See Charles Tart, *Waking Up* (Boston: Shambhala, 1987), 115–29.

23. Rainer Maria Rilke, "Annunciation to Mary," *Translations from the Poetry of Rainer Maria Rilke*, trans. M. D. Herter Norton (New York: W. W. Norton & Co., 1962), 201.

24. Annie Dillard, "God in the Doorway," *Teaching a Stone to Talk* (New York: Harper & Row, 1982), 141.

25. Frances Vaughan, *The Inward Arc* (Boston: Shambhala, 1986), 191; italics mine.

26. Eugene LaVerdiere, "Mary, Mother and Servant of the Lord," *Catholic Evangelization* (November/December 1988): 40–41.

27. Reginald H. Fuller, "A Note of Luke 1:28 and 38," *The New Testament Age*, ed. William C. Weinrich (Macon, Ga.: Mercer University Press, 1984), 205.

28. Dennis McFarland, *The Music Room* (Boston: Houghton Mifflin Company, 1990), 94–95.

29. *Luther's Works*, ed. J. Pelikan (St. Louis: Concordia, 1956), 21:299.

Quoted in Charles Talbert, *Reading Luke* (New York: Crossroad, 1982), 21.

30. Frederick Sontag, "The Spiritual Connection," *Religious Studies and Theology* 8, no. 3 (September 1988): 12.

31. Denise Levertov, *A Door in the Hive* (New York: New Directions, 1989).

32. Quoted in Kenneth Voiles, "The Importance of Mary in the Spirituality of Thomas Merton," *Spiritual Life* 36, no. 4 (Winter 1990): 223.

Chapter 5: The Magi Ride Again

1. Raymond Brown, *The Birth of the Messiah* (New York: Doubleday, 1977), 198.

2. Although people tend to contrast the functions of history and fiction, the purposes of historical narrative and fictional narrative often considerably overlap. See Paul Ricoeur, "The Narrative Function," *Semeia* 13 (1978): 176–202.

3. See Raymond Brown, *The Birth of the Messiah*, 165–201.

4. I could not find the original essay. This rendition of it is indebted to Fulton Sheen, *Christmas Inspirations* (New York: Maco Publications, 1966), 32.

5. G. K. Chesterton, *Collected Poems* (New York: Dodd, Mead & Company, 1932), 127–28.

6. Ibid., 129.

7. Quoted in *In the Spirit of Wonder*, ed. M. L. Shrady (New York: Pantheon Books, 1961), 81.

8. William Butler Yeats, "The Magi," in *Poems of Christmas*, ed. Myra Cohn Livingston (New York: Atheneum, 1980), 20.

9. *T. S. Eliot: The Collected Poems, 1909–1962* (New York: Harcourt, Brace & World, 1963), 99.

10. Henry Van Dyke, *The Story of the Other Wise Man* (New York: Harper & Brothers, 1923).

11. *Religious Drama* (New York: Meridian, 1957).

12. Quoted in *The Oxford Book of Christmas Poems* (New York: University Press, 1983), 55–56.

13. Quoted in *Poems of Christmas*, ed. Myra Cohn Livingston (New York: Atheneum, 1980), 84.

14. G. K. Chesterton, *The Spirit of Christmas* (New York: Dodd, Mead \& Company, 1985), 49.

15. Quoted in Jean Thoburn, *Away in a Manger* (New York: David McKay Co.).

16. John Shea, "Epiphany in Doubt," unpublished.

Chapter 6: The Close and Holy Darkness

1. Quoted in Alan W. Jones, "The Visibility of Christ and the Affliction of Transcendence," in *Spirit and Light* (New York: Seabury Press, 1976), 124.

2. J. Lewis May, *Father Tyrrell and the Modernist Movement* (London: Eyre and Spottiswoode, 1932).

3. Incarnation is also a spiritual process. We have explored the elements of this process in chapter 2 above.

4. J. Barrie Shepherd, "The Silent Seers," quoted in *Weavings* 3, no. 6 (November/December 1988): 24–25.

5. Quoted by Robert Granat, "THE *nevertheless* RELIGION," *The Roll: Newsletter of the Schola Contemplationis* (September 1988).

6. Alan Watts, *The Two Hands of God* (New York: George Braziller, 1963), 168.

7. C. S. Lewis, *A Grief Observed* (London: Faber \& Faber, 1961), 59.

8. James Joyce, "The Dead," *Dubliners* (Mineola, N.Y.: Dover, 1991), 152.

9. William Shannon, "Thomas Merton and the Quest for Self-Identity," *Cistercian Studies* 22, no. 2 (1987): 172.

10. Viktor Frankl, *Man's Search for Meaning* (New York: Washington Square, 1963), 63–64; quoted in Justin J. Kelley, "Knowing by Heart: The Symbolic Structure of Revelation and Faith," in *Faithful Witness*, ed. Leo O'Donovan and T. Howland Sanks (New York: Crossroad, 1989), 74.

11. Ram Dass, *Grist for the Mill* (Berkeley: California: Celestial Arts, 1976), 116.

12. Gabriel Marcel. *The Mystery of Being II: Faith and Reality* (Chicago: Henry Regnery Company, 1960), 171.

13. C. S. Lewis, *A Grief Observed*, 57, 58, 59.

14. Allan Jones, *Passion for Pilgrimage* (San Francisco: Harper & Row, 1989); quoted in *The Daybook: A Contemplative Journal* (Winter 1991–92).

15. Denise Levertov, "St. Peter and the Angel," *Oblique Prayers* (New York: New Directions, 1984), 79.

16. See Raymond Brown, *The Birth of the Messiah* (New York: Doubleday, 1977), 403–5.

OTHER STORY RESOURCES

Gospel Food for Hungry Christians
Matthew, Mark, Luke and John
JOHN SHEA

This series of audio tapes offers a unique view into each of the four Gospels. It brings scripture, spirituality and theology together in new, refreshing and rewarding ways. (Four separate sets of six audio cassette tapes, $29.95 each)

The Man on the Ox and Other Tales
The Antique Watch and Other Tales
JOHN SHEA

Two separate video tape programs, each containing nine of John Shea's favorite stories told by professional actors, with commentary after each by Shea himself. (Two separate 40-minute VHS video tapes, $29.95 each)

Christmas Presence
Twelve Gifts That Were More Than They Seemed
EDITED BY GREGORY F. AUGUSTINE PIERCE

Winner of a Catholic Press Association 2003 Book Award. This bestselling collection of stories about Christmas gifts that revealed the presence of God includes John Shea's "The Christmas Kaleidoscope." (160-page hardcover with gift ribbon, $17.95)

Hidden Presence
Twelve Blessings That Transformed Sorrow or Loss
EDITED BY GREGORY F. AUGUSTINE PIERCE

Twelve original stories about how grace can flow from sadness. A hopeful book for those who believe that God is with us, even in our darkest hours. Includes Joyce Rupp's "The Gift My Brother Gave Me." (176-page hardcover with gift ribbon, $17.95)

Running into the Arms of God
Stories of Prayer/Prayer as Story
PATRICK HANNON, CSC

Stories of prayer in everyday life tied to the traditional hours of the monastic day: matins, lauds, prime, terce, sext, none, vespers, compline. Winner of the first place award in the 2006 Catholic Press Association Book Awards for the first time author of a book. (128-page hardcover, $15.95; paperback $11.95)

Available from booksellers or call 800-397-2282
(www.actapublications.com)